MORE
THAN
>
JUST
SURVIVING
One Woman's Journey

Denise Royal

ISBN 978-1-63814-962-0 (Paperback)
ISBN 978-1-63814-963-7 (Digital)

Covenant Books
11661 Hwy 707
Murrells Inlet, SC 29576
www.covenantbooks.com

As my loving Lord God instructs me to write this book, He guides me to portray Him as The Forester in the first chapters. Throughout the rest of the book, He asks me to depict Him as Maestro of the Grand Orchestra.

I use my imagination trying to make these images congeal, but my mind can't get them to connect.

Lord, I don't understand.
The two items don't fit together!
Please show me how I can be both a tree in a forest and a musician!

He tenderly whispers,

"You are not a musician.
you are an instrument in My orchestra.
I, The Forester,
grow you, My tree.
At the perfect time, I harvest you.
then fashion your lumber into an instrument.
You are part of My orchestra bringing Me glory."

Pausing, I humbly bow.
Wow.
I get it. I finally understand.
You're incredible!

SYMPHONY
INCEPTION

1

The alarm clock on my night table begins softly playing Christian music, the melody signals a new day. "Good morning!" the radio DJ announces. "Hope you've made plans for the weekend! The weather should be spectacular! Get out there and enjoy yourselves!"

I eagerly open my eyes, anticipating the coming weekend. *Get up and get going! Got to be ready by two forty-five for the women's seminar! Leslie will be here around three o'clock. My two other friends will be here by three fifteen!*

My right hand hits the alarm clock off button. Stealthily, I stretch and grab my robe. *I love springtime in the Rockies! I can't wait to see what new beginnings and changes this year will bring!*

I glance at my sleeping husband and continue tip-toeing toward our bedroom door. *Thank You, Lord, for this man! Help him get the sleep he needs to be sharp before he starts his evening shift on the police department.* Quietly, I shut the door behind me.

There is no way I can know this very weekend will prepare me for the most difficult trial of my life. The enemy places his snare. Now he lurks, waiting for the disaster to unfold. I have no idea that my life's about to forever pivot, making me question everything I know. As I make my way past our kids' rooms, I stop at each portal to get our two kids moving. "John, Shannon, time to wake up!" I wait until I see covers tussle. My eight-year-old son yawns. His sister, six, stretches. "Good morning, sleepyheads! I'll see you in the kitchen!"

I grab a skillet, eggs, and bread to cook breakfast. Both children soon enter our cozy country kitchen, rubbing eyes and buttoning shirts.

"Breakfast's ready. Have a seat! John, will you say our breakfast prayer?"

He nods. "Thank you, God, for this food. Be with me and Shannon at school. Amen."

"Thanks, John. Now, both of you hurry and eat so you won't be late for school." They gobble down their meals then jostle to the bathroom to brush their teeth.

I rally my small troop, "It's time to go!" We begin our five-block walk to the elementary school. I kiss each blond head as I turn to leave. "Remember, I'm going to the women's meeting tonight. Carol will pick you up from school and stay with you till Dad gets home. I'll be back tomorrow night. Love you!"

I spend the rest of my day making my family's dinner and cleaning the house. *Okay, now make sure the car is clean. Pack for tonight: Bible, gown, robe, toothbrush, makeup, and notebook!* I glance at the clock.

Perfect! Finished just in time! There's Leslie! I grab my bag and lock the door as I close it behind me.

"Good to see you! The others should be here any minute!" The words are barely out of my mouth when they both pull up. "Let's go!" Like schoolgirls, the four of us pile into my vehicle giggling and chatting with excitement. We rarely get away from our homes and daily responsibilities.

Lord, I can't wait to experience your Spirit move in our hearts! I hope my friends enjoy the conference as much as I did last year! The sun streaming through the car windows enhances our happy-go-lucky, bright outlooks.

*****

We safely arrive at the hotel, briefly settle into our room, and then rush to a fast-food restaurant nearby. We laugh while gulping down our meals, then quickly return to the hotel for the meetings that are about to start.

God speaks to my heart almost as soon as the first speaker starts sharing. He reveals areas where I need to make changes, as well as those I need to release into His capable hands. Back in our room, the four of us stay up late sharing what God said to each of us.

As I lie back on the pillow, I pray, *Lord, I don't know what You have in store for my future. Help me remain faithful to You. I know You will work everything out. After all, I'm faithful to You. No difficulties too great will enter my life.* I smugly snuggle into a deep sleep.

Conferences resume early the next morning. The out-of-state speakers challenge us. At the end of the last session, the lead speaker announces, "You've been given both a card and an envelope stamped with the weekend motto: 'Be All God Wants You to Be.' Please take this time to write what God told you this weekend. Pray over your statement. Seal it in the envelope. Hide this envelope somewhere in your house when you get home."

God shows me one particular thing to jot down. *Lord, I don't really understand why You're telling me to write that since I'm pretty sure I'm already doing it.* Submitting, I write it down and seal it in the envelope.

Thirty-six hours after we'd arrived, the four of us head home physically exhausted from lack of sleep, yet spiritually refreshed by the incredible teaching. During the quiet ride, individually we contemplate what we learned as I drive our transformed group back home.

I arrive in a dreamy sleep-deprived state, looking forward to seeing my husband, my anchor of hope. *I love this man! He constantly looks for ways to help around the house and with our kids. He's naturally upbeat, rarely in a bad mood. He daily compliments and encourages me. At least once a day he tells me he loves me. I can't believe we'll celebrate our ninth anniversary in a couple of months! Life can't get much better!*

As I step into our kitchen, I see my hubby. *Just as I expected, here he is, helping me with housework!* Jamie turns from where he stands, hands dripping dishwater. "Hi, baby! Welcome home!" His arms open, welcoming me toward him for a soapy hug. Instantly, I feel the familiar loving warmth of our home. I smile, step forward, and lean into his embrace. *Thank You, Lord, for my family!*

Later that afternoon, I kiss my husband as he leaves for his swing shift.

My roots anchor deeply, my trunk towers broadly, my foliage spreads beautifully dense.

2

After Jamie pulls out of the driveway, I begin unpacking. *Okay, dirty clothes in the hamper, books on the shelf, Bible on the nightstand, makeup, and toothbrush in the bathroom. That should do it.*

A bit of colored paper at the bottom of my overnight bag catches my eye. *Oh! My commitment card! Where should I put you?*

I glance around my room as the backdoor slams shut. *This needs to go someplace special.* I hear John and Shannon race through the house toward my room. *Better hurry! The natives are getting restless!* My hand quickly grabs the card. I kneel and bury it under clothes in my dresser drawer. *Whew, just in time!*

Later that evening, I kiss each downy head as I put the kids to bed. *Ah, it's great to be home! Now that the kids are tucked in for the night, I can relax.* My musings cause me to recount my life's journey.

Growing up in a nomadic military family meant living with constant changes. This kept me excitedly anticipating new adventures. Dad was an Air Force fighter pilot who humbly served our country for twenty years. My parents had twenty-five moves under their belts. I loved being the "baby" of the family, in a girl-boy-girl pattern.

I lived in a "father knows best" or "leave it to beaver" world. Mom and Dad gave peck kisses on cheeks to each other, often holding hands when sitting close on a couch. My parents were wonderful examples of godly living. They showed love for all through manners and respect. They exemplified Philippians 4:8 (NIV), "Finally, brothers, whatever is true, whatever is noble, whatever is right, whatever is pure, whatever is lovely, whatever is admirable—if anything is excellent or praiseworthy—think about such things." I only remember a couple of times when they made a negative comment about another person and raising their voices toward each other once. My childhood was laced with love and laughter.

Dad was off work almost every national holiday. On these occasions, he and Mom asked families from our church over for a party. Dad usually grilled out for summer affairs. Mom fixed fresh lemonade and iced sweet tea. They made everyone feel welcome. Mom decorated the house for every event: Fourth of July was of course red, white, and blue streamers, balloons, napkin rings, and homemade tablecloths. She planned the menu, as well as decorated a cake to match each event. Anyone new to our area was invited to our house for these occasions.

Our daily routine was simple. Mom woke us up on weekdays singing a silly song. After a prayer and breakfast, we went to school. Mom greeted us with a smile and often a plate of warm homemade cookies when we arrived home each day. Easy listening music played softly on our stereo as we gobbled down the delights. We'd then scurry outside to play. While in California, I'd catch butterflies with the net Mom made from a clothes hanger and netting.

When we lived on a military base, we'd hear the national anthem play over loudspeakers at 4:30 p.m. Everyone on base either stood at attention or froze in place, quickly bringing their right hand over their heart. Once the song finished, we raced to our front door. The song was our signal to get home. Dad's workday was finished; he was on his way home. When he arrived, we sat around our dinner table and held hands. Before each meal, Dad called on one of us to lead the family in prayer. We rarely made it through a meal without bursting into peals of laughter. Nothing was really that funny; life was just that good.

After dinner, we did our homework. If we all finished early enough, we played a board game. Afterward, one of our parents read a bedtime story. Dad and Mom tucked us each snugly into our beds with a prayer and a kiss on our forehead.

On weekends, we gathered around our kitchen table to play board games. Much of the time a jigsaw puzzle was scattered across an extra table. Our one television was rarely watched.

Whenever I wasn't at school, I observed Mom's afternoon routine. She made sure her hair looked nice, reapplied makeup, and changed into a clean set of clothes. As I became a teenager, she instructed me, "Make sure you look nice for your husband when he gets home. Greet him with a kiss at the door after his long day at work."

Mom took Friday nights "off." Dad and us kids made Chef Boyardee pizza. Because this was the only night we were allowed to drink soda and watch TV during a meal, we ate in our den on TV trays! Dad didn't cook a huge variety of things, but his popcorn, pizza, beanie-weenies, hamburgers, and hot dogs were spectacular!

Occasionally, silliness overtook my folks. Dad raced through a room laughing, tears rolling down his cheeks. Mom was in close pursuit! Cindy, Roger, and I glanced at each other, shrugged, and grinned. *Here they go again!*

We never knew what started these episodes. The result, however, was inevitable. Dad laughed so hard he was unable to run any further. He collapsed on the floor. Mom pounced on top of him, proudly the victor. She perched on Dad's chest as they both laughed hysterically.

*****

After twenty years in the military, Dad's career was complete. He retired. We packed our things.

Here we go again. Lord, out of all our moves, this one's the hardest! I'm fifteen and this is my thirteenth move! I thought leaving Okinawa was difficult, but not like this! I know moving is our family "normal," but right now, it stinks! I sighed. Oh well, better face the facts. Life goes on. I knew to expect it. It is what it is. I'll finish high school wherever we end up. Dad says he and Mom will know when we get there. I'm pretty much all right with that. You've always been faithful. Dad and

Mom have a close relationship with You. I may as well settle in "for the ride." We left Maine after a huge snow storm. Our family formed a caravan. Dad shepherded his little flock driving our family vehicle. It was packed with essentials we'd need until we got settled: clothes, plates, cups, utensils, and a couple of pans. The car's other occupants were Mom's houseplants, drinking water, and snacks. Attached to his car was our family's pop-up tent trailer. Cindy and I followed in her Datsun. Mom and Roger trailed in Dad's Toyota.

Because Cindy and Roger were both out of high school, we stopped in Oklahoma to leave them and Cindy's vehicle with relatives. Dad, Mom, and I pressed onward, continuing west. My parents were compelled to go to Colorado.

Passing the "Welcome to Colorado" sign, Mom and I cheered. "Hooray!" We drove through Longmont. *I could live here.* We continued through Greeley, Denver, and then into Colorado Springs. Each time my mind echoed the sentiment. *Yep, this place could do.* When we drove to Woodland Park, my brow furrowed as we drove by the school. *What a bunch of hicks! I hate this place.*

Mom and Dad's excitement grew as we toured the tiny town. "This is it!" they declared with broad grins.

No! I slunk lower and lower in the back seat. By the end of the week Mom and Dad rented our next home: a fourteen-by-sixty-foot trailer. *We've hit rock bottom. Dad doesn't have a job, and we're living in a trailer park next to the sewer plant.*

My parents immediately enrolled me in the town high school. *Here I am again…the new kid at another school, middle of the year. Great!* After finishing paperwork in the school office, I entered the American History class. The diminutive male teacher was midsentence. "Yes. Can I help you?" All eyes peered at me as the class became deathly silent. *Everyone's curiously sizing me up.*

"I'm Denise Pattison. I just moved here and was assigned to your class."

"Where'd you move from?"

"Maine."

"Maine? Why did you move?"

"Well, my dad retired from the service. My parents decided to live here."

"What branch of the service?"

I proudly answered, "Air Force."

"The Air Force!" he thundered. "I was a Marine!" the drill sergeant pointed as he bellowed. "Go sit in that chair in the back corner!"

Flushed, I lowered my head. My shoulders and head fell. I shuffled past gawking eyes. *How small can I make myself? At least I was ordered to sit behind everyone!*

The rest of the morning was better. *Thankfully, the other teachers weren't rude.*

At lunch, a girl asked, "Do you want to eat with me and my friends?"

"Sure. Thanks."

The gaggle of girls asked repeated questions throughout the meal. *It's a different town, but the same routine. Take notes on the new kid.* "Where'd you move from? What do your parents do? Do you have an older brother?" Once I hit junior high, they didn't care that I have a sister; they were very intrigued to know about Roger.

Then came the question that separated me from most other kids. "Do you want to go to a party Friday night?"

"Sure. Where is it?"

"It's at my house," one girl volunteered. "We'll have tons of fun. My parents are leaving town for the weekend. I've invited the handsome jocks. One guy is even bringing a keg of beer!"

"Thanks for inviting me. I don't think I'll make it. I don't drink."

"Don't drink? Never mind. Don't bother coming." Giggles echoed. Elbows tapped ribs.

Oh, well. Tomorrow I'll find another group to sit with. I survived the rest of the first day.

Following our normal routine, our family immediately joined a local church. I met several kids I recognized from school. I started eating lunch with them the following week.

Roger and Cindy soon joined us. The two-bedroom trailer became tight with five of us. Cindy and I shared the master bedroom; Roger got the closet-sized extra room. Dad and Mom slept on a fold-up couch in the living room.

Several months later, Dad and Mom signed papers to buy our next house. Dad contacted the air force to deliver our furniture. My family settled into the new environment. Overnight, Mom had pictures on the walls and curtains over the windows.

While Roger waited for his high school diploma to arrive, he was hired at a local gas station. Cindy enrolled in school to become a Medical Assistant. *Her laughter and singing always reflected joy. Her extroverted personality consistently brought new friends into our lives. It was great to have everyone together again!*

The youth group became my second family. I took on leadership roles and soon sang in both the adult and youth choirs. The following fall, I joined the drama and puppet teams.

After we moved to Colorado, Cindy and I became close friends. For the first time in my life, the five-and-a-half-year age difference didn't matter. She and I shared common ideas, opinions, and interests. We both joined the church's adult choir. We sang together constantly.

Cindy kept in contact with her high school sweetheart, Jeff. He'd joined the air force as a military police officer. He was currently stationed in England. Jeff's duty assignment was due to change locations in January. His orders were to be stationed at the same base where Dad had been assigned in Maine. The summer following my junior year, he proposed to Cindy. My heart played tug-of-war. I was so excited for Cindy! I knew I would miss her! I wondered how I'd manage without her? In January, Jeff flew from England to Colorado. The two got married at our church. Within days, they packed Cindy's car and drove to Maine.

Life without Cindy was subdued, lonely, and horribly quiet. Dad and Roger rarely spoke. At least Mom and I bantered back and forth over evening meals.

One evening during family dinner, Mom asked, "Denise, I read in the paper about a sign language class at Colorado Springs School for the Deaf and Blind. Do you want to go?"

"Well, it's all the way in the Springs. I'd have to borrow your car."

"I thought I'd take the class with you! We'll ride together!"

"I didn't know you're interested in signing."

"You bet I am! I love learning new things!"

Mom and I enrolled. One evening a week we attended the class.

The Forester smiled as He gently placed the seed
upon the rich soil;
Then He waited patiently for roots to take hold.

*****

The summer between my junior and senior year of high school, I attended our church's youth camp. During the last evening's service, God convicted me. "You need to become a Christian. Ask Me into your life. Surrender to Me. Make Me the Lord of your life." Yielding to His prompting, I went forward during an invitation. The counselor queried, "How can I help you?"

Timidly, I answered, "I don't know if I'm a Christian. I want to ask Jesus into my life."

"Denise, I know all you do in the church. I know you're a Christian. You just need to rededicate your life to the Lord."

"Okay." *I don't think you're right, but if you say so...* I bowed my head and prayed, "God help me be a better Christian."

Doubts continued to plague me after I arrived home. *I don't know what's wrong with my walk with God. The people I respect most have intimate relationships with Him. I can't seem to get close to Him.* Unrelenting questions about my relationship with God flooded my mind. I began to pray regularly, "God, if I'm not saved, save me."

Our youth pastor's wife, Marilyn Cheek, asked, "Could I disciple you? We'd meet weekly. I'll show you new ways to study the

Bible. We'll memorize scriptures together and share what God speaks to us about! Does that sound like something you'd like to do?"

"Absolutely!"

We scheduled our meeting times and days. *I loved this time with her. There's only one problem; every time Marilyn tells me what God showed her, but God's not speaking to me! Maybe next week I'll get a word from Him.*

I prayed and studied harder. Week after week… I heard nothing. *Marilyn's spiritual walk is so different than mine! God's remarkably active in her life! God seems like her best friend. Each week God gives her fresh insight. In contrast, my quiet time with God is stale, barren. Her walk's steadfast and strong. It must be like in school—some kids don't have to study as much as I do. Things just come naturally for them. I'll just work harder than ever!*

Our church was exciting! People accepted Christ as their Savior weekly. Church members regularly gave testimonies of God's faithfulness. *I easily see God at work in lives all around me. But something's missing from my spiritual walk. I feel hollow inside. My relationship with God falls flat when I compare their lives with mine.*

During the spring of my high school senior year, my church invited a special speaker. Members were asked to go to the church and fill time slots to pray for the upcoming event. The hope was to pray "around the clock" for several days before the guest speaker arrived. Proudly, I volunteered and dutifully went to the church at my allotted time. *After all, that's what the people whose lives are right with God do.* My pastor recently spoke about being transparent before God. I honestly pleaded. *God, if there's anything in my life that isn't real, anything that needs to be revealed, show me!*

That Sunday, the guest pastor talked about the sick people whom Jesus healed. He shared how they knew they were sick and needed healing. God touched my heart and I saw my problem. *For years, I've been unwilling to admit to God that I need Him. I've always said, "If I need You…"* Now I know I need Him and His forgiveness! The preacher ended the service with an invitation for anyone who needed Jesus in their life to raise their hand. Mine went up immediately. Then he asked those who raised their hand to come forward and speak with a counselor. My heart pounded. *I can't do that! Everyone knows all the positions I hold in the church! Everyone believes I'm already a Christian!*

The congregation stood. My fingers tightly clenched the pew in front of me. As the congregation sang the second verse, I finally surrendered. As I sobbed, I made my way toward my pastor. I talked in a separate room with a counselor and prayed. "Lord, forgive my sin. Thank You for Jesus! Thank You that He died to pay the punishment for my sin. Lord, please make me Your child. Be my Lord!" Peace immediately flooded my soul. Calm unlike any I had ever known filled my entire being. I knew I was now God's child!

Afterward, I became filled with an insatiable appetite for God's Word. I wasn't studying the Bible just to complete a book, check the right box, or get the right answers. I was studying to become closer to God, to hear Him speak fresh words to my heart. I came to church with fresh enthusiasm to learn real-life heart knowledge of God. Week after week, as the preacher proclaimed the message, I sat on the edge of my seat, like a flower leaned toward the brightness and warmth of the sun.

God, the nurturing Forester, rejoiced.
The seed He planted took root and burst through the soil!

SYMPHONY MOVEMENT NO. 1

3

I graduated from high school a few months after accepting Jesus as my Lord and Savior. The last two years were rough as I struggled with intermittent, horrible headaches, and bouts of dizziness. Doctors gave no answers for the cause of my illness. I ignored all this and was filled with youthful optimism. The future still looked bright.

Summer passed quickly. Roger moved to Colorado Springs. The house was quieter than ever. My friends headed off to college. Because of my health issues, I decided not to go to college. Autumn gradually turned to winter. I didn't know what You wanted me to do. *God, I'm lonely, confused and discouraged.* I prayed earnestly. *God, please show me Your plans!* I spent most of my days cleaning my parents' house, cooking, and playing their piano.

As Christmas approached, I threw myself into practicing for the church's musical. *It'd be gorgeous. This was my first Christmas as a believer! Every word of every Christmas song filled me with an excitement that I'd never experienced! I'd had the real meaning of Christmas living inside me! The lyrics were alive! My heart felt like it couldn't contain so much joy!*

The night of the Christmas musical arrived. My enemy, fatigue, was back. I won't be in the choir tonight after all. I was too exhausted to participate, but I knew I'd still enjoy the performance.

Dad drove Mom and me to our church. As I walked down the center aisle, a familiar man's voice boomed my name. "Denise! Denise! Come here! I want you to meet my son, Jamie!" Just as I expected, it was Mr. Royal. Sitting by him were his wife and a young man. Mr. Royal was stationed with my dad in California fifteen years earlier. Recently, my church voted for him to be our church's mission pastor in Cripple Creek. As family friends, he and his wife were often guests in my parents' home. Each time they came, they recognized my cooking abilities and told me, "You've got to meet our son!" They repeated the same script each time I saw them: "Our son is young, single, and very sweet." Now Mr. Royal announced, "This is our son, Jamie!" We shook hands. *So here he was…okay.* I inwardly shrugged. I continued walking forward closer to the front of the sanctuary.

The service was beautifully uplifting. Afterward, the church had a dessert time in the fellowship hall. As I stood, plate in hand, Jamie approached. We visited easily. He was nice. Then the lights went out! *This was awkward!* My heart thundered! Some kid had bumped the light switch. It took a moment before an adult turned it back on. With the room illuminated once again, I saw Jamie's smiling face and our conversation continued. He laughed loudly and easily. All too soon it was time to go home. *Oh, well. I enjoyed the few minutes we spent together.* I inwardly shrugged as he left.

The next afternoon, Jamie was visiting his parents for Christmas. Since my pastor and his wife were good friends with Jamie's family, they were having a meal together. My name came up in conversation as they visited. My pastor's wife dialed my number, and quickly thrust the phone toward Jamie.

Our phone rang. Mom was upstairs and answered it. "Denise!" she sang, "It's for you!"

I curiously picked up the downstairs receiver, "Hello?"

"I can't believe I'm doing this!" a male voice stammered.

"That's okay…hmmm…what are you doing?" I asked.

He chuckled nervously. "This is Jamie Royal. I, uh, was wondering what you're doing tonight!"

"Well…it's Christmas Eve and I'm spending the night with my family and friends," I said with a smile. *I enjoyed the game of acting innocent, making the potential suitors squirm.*

"Oh…okay…bye!" he humbly stated. We both hung up.

Immediately, Mom raced down the stairs. "Who was it? What did he want?" She smiled feigning innocence.

"That was Jamie Royal. He wanted to know what I was doing tonight."

"What'd you tell him?"

"I told him it's Christmas Eve and we're having company."

Horrified, she demanded, "Call him back and ask him over! Here's the phone number!"

This was the day of neither cell phones nor private phone companies; long-distance calls were very expensive. "Mom, the call is long distance!" I explained, rolling my eyes.

"I'll pay for it!" she hastily countered.

While Mom made her way back upstairs, I hesitantly dialed the number. Jamie answered the phone. "I can't believe I'm doing this!" I stated, copying his opening remarks.

"That's okay," he laughed again.

"Can you come over and celebrate Christmas Eve with us?"

"I sure can!"

Three of our other guests were my close friend, Suzanne, and her parents. Her dad was a retired police officer; mine, a retired air force pilot. Suzanne said she would never marry a cop. I said I would never marry anyone in the military. It was our little joke. All evening the questions went on and on as Suzanne's dad fired them off at Jamie.

"Where do you work?"

"I'm on the sheriff's department in Garfield County."

"How much do you get paid? How long have you been there?" The questions were triggered off for what seemed like hours. After each answer, Suzanne jabbed me in the ribs and whispered comments. "He can afford you! He has good insurance! He has his own place!"

Suzanne, please! I'm sure he can hear you! I blushed crimson.

Just then, Mom began a one-person parade carrying trays of food into the den. "Denise cooked this!" she exclaimed repeatedly as she brought item after item into the den. With each additional entrée, I grew redder.

Mom, please stop! I'm going to die of embarrassment!

Time passed quickly. Suzanne and her family went home. Mom and Dad went to bed. Jamie and I stayed up for hours talking and laughing. We enjoyed our time together. We laughed about little, insignificant things, but also talked deeply of our spiritual lives, hopes, dreams, and expectations. Too soon I walked him to the door. The moment at the door was awkward. *I didn't know how to tell him goodbye. He seemed nervous as well.* Slowly he reached over and gently took my hand in his. He lifted my hand to his lips as though holding a precious jewel. Then he gently kissed the back of my hand. My heart melted; knees became weakened. *Stand up, girl! Breathe!* Then he was gone. He had to be back at his job four hours away, tomorrow.

*****

All night I couldn't stop thinking about Jamie. In the early hours, I finally drifted off to sleep. I awoke a couple of hours later to my first Christmas as a believer. *Wow! What an awesome day!* Everything was so new and alive! I spent the day with my parents, brother, and a few of Mom and Dad's friends. All day, I remembered the previous night. *Wonder if Jamie's home yet. Would I hear from him again?*

Five days after Jamie and I met, I prayed while vacuuming our downstairs. Suddenly, I heard a voice loudly speak to me. I knew instantly it was my Lord. I doubted that anyone else heard. "Denise, you've been asking Me what you're going to do with your life. You're going to marry Jamie."

The shock of what God said hit me full force. I plopped onto the couch. *You're right. I am.*

Jamie called later that day. I wanted so badly to say, "Guess what! We're going to get married!" but I managed to hold my tongue.

Jamie and I continued calling each other. Again, these were the days when long-distance charges were at an all-time high. We planned for me to accompany his parents for the four-hour drive to see him in a couple of weeks. I would stay in his extra bedroom. His parents would sleep in the living room on the hide-a-bed sofa.

22

Of course, he'd sleep in his own bedroom. We agreed to talk once a week until then.

Time crept sluggishly by! How can a few weeks feel like a decade? Finally, the date arrived! *I leave today!* I anxiously peered out the living room window as I waited for Mr. and Mrs. Royal to pick me up. Finally, they pulled into my parent's driveway! I grabbed my things and bounded out the door. Mr. Royal opened the trunk for my luggage. I climbed in the back seat. Unable to control my nerves, I chatted incessantly.

We arrived at Jamie's place four hours later. The neighborhood was well kept and quiet. As I got out of the car, the wafting scent of pine trees greeted me. To my shock, his parents went straight in his trailer without knocking. They called out, "Jamie, we're here!"

Complete silence greeted us. Jamie wasn't there. His place was as neat as it was empty. My heart sank. I suddenly felt very young and out of place. Inside, my emotions screamed!

What were you thinking? You think some guy five years older than you would be interested in you? You're crazy! He probably has a girlfriend. Now what are you going to do all weekend? You're stuck! Satan jostled my mind and emotions. Jamie's parents spoke freely, they laughed as time crept by. I tried to control my thoughts.

The minutes dragged on. Even the clock seemed to tick in slow motion. Suddenly Jamie kicked the front door open. His arms cradled groceries, his face beamed a wonderful smile. He set the groceries onto the kitchen counter, walked around the table to where I was sitting. He gently placed his hand on my shoulder and tenderly squeezed. "I'm so glad you came," he softly announced. Pleasant butterflies fluttered in my stomach.

Over the dinner Terri brought, I stated, "I like your trailer."

Jamie shared, "My last roommate, Jack, moved to California. He was on the sheriff's department too. I'm looking for another roommate to help with the rent."

He's looking for a roommate! I recalled Suzanne's elbow tapping my ribs on Christmas Eve.

That evening, we all went swimming at the local hot springs. Jamie chuckled as my permed hair kinked into tight ringlets across the back of my head. We talked and laughed together until our hands were as wrinkled as prunes. His parents swam easily and were considerate enough to occasionally give us some time alone.

When we got back to his trailer, Jamie immediately asked, "Do you want to go bowling?"

"Sure!" I replied.

"No," his parents answered. "We're tired and just want to stay here and relax. You kids go."

After arriving at the alley, we bowled a couple of games. He was a good bowler. I barely broke one hundred points, but gave him good reason for more laughter. After a few games, we headed back to the trailer. Jamie's parents soon went to bed. He and I stayed up half the night talking. "If it's not raining in the morning, we'll go skiing," Jamie excitedly stated.

I gulped hard. *I'd never been skiing. I was totally uncoordinated, terrified of heights, and was already completely exhausted.* I went to bed that night praying for rain. I prayed hard and earnestly. I barely slept. When I awoke the next morning, I glanced outside. *Rain! Glorious rain! Thank You, God! You answered my prayers!*

After greeting Jamie and his parents at the breakfast table, I smugly proclaimed, "It's raining..."

"Yeah," Jamie pondered, "but I'll call the ski slope. It's often snowing there when it's raining here."

Oh my. I shuddered.

"Sure enough, the conditions at the slope are excellent!" Jamie beamed broadly. So off to the slopes he and I plowed ahead! Jamie helped me get into my short, stubby, heavy, rented skis. He showed me how to stop by pointing my skis together. With Jamie's idea of skiing instruction completed, we plodded toward the lift. Waddle, waddle, waddle, kerplunk...waddle, waddle, waddle, kerplunk. I took two or three steps and fell, two or three steps and fell.

Before I knew it, we were at the lift. Suddenly we were airborne! Looking down at the mountainside, I trembled in fear. When we got to the top, my mittens were soaked with perspiration. *I didn't know hands sweated!* I managed to get off the lift and skied a few feet. Kerplunk! I fell! All at once, everyone on the lift behind me dismounted and tried to maneuver around me. A few others fell also.

Oh, boy. Here we go, Grace. How do you pull off looking cool now?

Jamie helped me to my feet and laughed. *This man can do everything! Swim, bowl, ski…everything!*

"Don't put the pole straps around your wrists! You might hurt yourself if you fall!" he instructed. We started down the hill. *Wow! I made it fifteen feet before falling again!* As I fell, my arms flailed up and backward. Swoosh! There went the poles at least five feet behind me! I army crawled up the hill to my poles. I struggled to stand up. *There!* I felt proud of my ability to right myself. *Okay, let's try this again.*

Fifteen feet and swoosh! Kerplunk! This scene was repeated over and over until we were halfway down the mountain. Jamie was incredibly patient. He skied a few yards then waited for me to catch up. Each time I slid beside him he gave me a peck on my cheek. After my fifth or sixth fall, Jamie yelled up the hillside, "Put the straps around your wrists!"

"I thought I might hurt myself!" I countered back to him.

"Put the straps around your wrists!" an exasperated Jamie shouted.

Somehow, we made it to the mountain's base and back to the top again. The second run went mildly smoother. I didn't fall when I got off the lift. After we skied halfway down, I told him, "Why don't you go on. I'll make it down by myself, that way you can get in some real skiing."

"Are you sure? I don't mind waiting."

"Yeah, I'm sure. Go ahead."

As he headed out, I continued my shuffle, waddle, and kerplunk routine. After another awkward drop, I lay sprawled out on the snow, staring at the few wispy clouds overhead. I heard someone shout from the chairlift above, "Is this your first day?"

"How could you tell?" I yelled back, smiling. My head shook from side to side in embarrassment.

Then, before I knew it, the two-day trip ended. In a blink, we were back at Jamie's place. His parents had already loaded their car. They sat in their Subaru buckled up, this left Jamie and I alone to say our goodbyes.

Jamie, leaned forward, softly spoke three short words, "I love you." Then he kissed me.

My heart welled inside of me. *Oh my.* He was not the first man to tell me he loved me. He was the first I knew meant it. Things were moving much quicker than I imagined. I knew God told me that we were going to get married, but I thought things would unfold in maybe a year or two. *Oh my.* Overwhelmed, I swallowed hard and started to softly cry. Getting into his parents' car I remained completely silent.

We left without another comment between us. The long drive home was painfully awkward. Neither his parents nor I said a word. I sat completely silent, intermittently wiping a tear. His dad occasionally stole glances in the rearview mirror. *Oh my.*

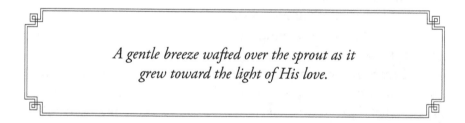

A gentle breeze wafted over the sprout as it grew toward the light of His love.

4

Jamie and I continued twice monthly phone conversations and wrote snail-mail letters. The more we conversed, the more I realized we had similar goals and dreams. I soon knew that I did indeed love him and "yes," wanted to spend the rest of my life with him. The next time we saw each other was right before Valentine's Day. I wanted to wait until February 14 to tell him. *That would be so romantic.*

As soon as he got off work on the morning of February 12, Jamie drove five hours over the mountain pass to my parents' house. *How will I be able to wait two days to tell him?*

On the first day, we went for a long walk. We talked about what we hoped for in the future, what we wanted in a spouse, how many children we hoped to have, our relationship with our Lord. Our hopes and goals were almost identical! I couldn't wait any longer! I had to tell him!

Slowly, I stopped walking. I looked deeply into his blue eyes, then softly stated, "Jamie, I love you!" His eyes lit up as a smile flashed across his face. We kissed deeply before continuing to walk the remainder of the way to my parents' home, hand in hand. We spoke of how much fun we had together.

When we got back to the house, we went downstairs to the den. Then he surprised me! He asked me to marry him! I excitedly responded with an immediate, emphatic, "Yes!"

A few hours later we drove to the closest town and picked out rings. We set the wedding date for August second.

Since we hadn't known each other long, and he was five years older, we weren't sure what my parents would say. We decided to wait a little bit before breaking the news to them.

That night, when Jamie arrived at his parents' house, my pastor and his family were playing a game. Jamie told them everything. They laughed and congratulated each other over being perfect "matchmakers."

When Jamie arrived at my home the next day, he told me about his loose lips. We decided to tell Dad and Mom before they heard about this from someone else.

That evening, as we sat in the family room with my parents, Jamie interrupted all conversation, "Pat, Alma, I need to talk with you."

"All right." They glanced at each other, nodded, and gulped. Mom stated, "Come upstairs."

Jamie and I followed them. I led Jamie to the living room couch. Both parents went into the kitchen, got glasses of water, and joined us.

Jamie was admittedly nervous. Being in law enforcement, and always prepared for an emergency, he never was without a gun. That evening was no different. He had one in the waistband of his pants. He slowly removed it and set the weapon on the couch beside him. He inhaled deeply, "I would like to ask you for permission to marry your daughter."

My parents instantly gave their consent. (I still laugh as I ponder if the gun influenced them!) They agreed on our wedding date, six months later.

Jamie visited me once a month. Regardless of the weather, he rode his motorcycle. Having driven over the Continental Divide, once inside my parents' house, after a much-anticipated kiss and hug, he turned his back to our hot woodburning stove. He remained there for almost half an hour, rubbing his hands together behind his back.

On every visit he took me to the best restaurant in the area. "Bring me a doggy bag!" Mom smiled and winked. We consistently ordered prime rib with an enormous bowl of chilled boiled shrimp. I believed he had to be fairly wealthy. (After our wedding, it didn't take me long to figure out he rode his motorcycle to save money!)

I anxiously counted the days until I received the promised diamond to place in my engagement ring. Two weeks later Mom drove me to the post office. There was a small box addressed to me! Tape securely held the precious contents.

I ran to the car, jumped in, and excitedly tore the package open. After a small struggle the treasure was finally freed. Mom quietly watched. I reached inside questioningly as I saw a small ball of toilet paper. Slowly, I unpeeled each layer. At last, I saw it. But...it... was...yellow...yellow diamond? I'd never seen a yellow diamond! My shoulders sagged in disappointment.

"Let me see!" Mom chirped, as she broadly grinned. I slowly opened my hand, fingers trembling. "How beautiful! It's so unique!" Mom commented. "Let's get right over to the jewelers and get that stone set!" I straightened my back. My shoulders relaxed.

*****

In March, I had an extra day off work and decided to visit Jamie. After work I walked two blocks to the bus station where I boarded the bus. I rode the bus to Glenwood Springs, Jamie's western slope town. The ride I expected to take five and a half hours, took ten.

The last time we spoke, Jamie gave me a number to call when I got to town. After unloading from the bus, I dialed the specified number on the sole payphone. A dispatcher's gruff female voice curtly answered, "Garfield County Sheriff's Department. Is this an emergency?"

"Uh, n-no," I stuttered.

"How can I help you?" she questioned.

"Well, uh... Jamie Royal works for you. Uh... I'm his fiancé. He told me to call this number when I got to town."

Like a chameleon changes colors, her voice changed to warmth that could melt butter. "Oh! Certainly! He mentioned you'd be calling. I'll let him know you called! Can I help with anything else?"

"No, but thanks." I'd never called a sheriff's department before.

Nervously, I chatted with other passengers as I waited. Suddenly, a police vehicle appeared. The lights flashed, siren screamed, as the cruiser grated to a stop on the dirt parking lot. People in the depot scurried; they crowded in front of the window.

Out of the police cruiser barreled my fiancé. He raced inside and gathered me into his arms. Laughing I readily returned his embrace. We exchanged a long-awaited kiss! I blushed deeply.

Jamie proudly escorted me to his patrol car and opened the passenger's door. Sheepishly I sat down and buckled myself. I wasn't used to being in the spotlight.

"We're going to the local diner, The M and M, or as we call it, 'The Maggot and Maggot,'" Jamie stated with a hearty laugh. "One of my coworkers will meet us there. His name is Mel. You'll like him. He's an older guy. He'll take you to my landlord's house. That's the place I told you that you could stay." He was scheduled to work till three tomorrow morning.

The diner was just a few blocks away from the bus depot. Jamie opened my car door and gallantly led me inside.

I like that I don't have to guess what he is thinking and that I don't have to eat at the "Maggot and Maggot."

The interior was typical for a diner with seats by a bar, a few tables, and an old Jukebox. A waitress, about Mom's age, seated us. She winked at Jamie. We were the only clients. "Karen, can I use your phone?" Jamie asked.

"Sure," the waitress replied.

Jamie walked to the phone by the cash register, dialed the number as the waitress handed me a menu. "Here you go. I'll be back in a minute. Can I get you anything to drink?"

"A Coke please," I softly stated. *Surely that will be safe!* Still anxious about the "Maggot and Maggot" comment, I inwardly shuddered.

Jamie returned and sat down after he adjusted his holster. "Mel said he'll be right here. You'll really like him. He's about our dads' ages. Both he and Cal retired from other jobs before they became

deputies. Cal is my landlord. His wife is Beverly. They're real sweet."
He laughed loudly. "I eat at their place at least five times a week.
They own the trailer court and apartments where I live."

"How was your bus ride?" Jamie continued.

"Slow! Dad and I drove over in five hours, not ten!"

"I thought you'd never get here! I'd been expecting a call!"

"Yeah. The bus stopped at every little town along the way!"

"Hey! Mel!" Jamie shouted as an older gentleman entered. I
turned and saw a man who smiled as he strolled toward us. "This
is my gal, Denise!" Jamie exclaimed as he stood. He hugged Mel,
leaned down to hug and kiss me as he said, "Well, gotta run! See you
in the morning!" Then he was out the door.

Mel asked, "Would you like anything to eat?"

"Uh, no, I'm fine with the Coke. Thanks." Thoughts of Jamie's
nickname for this place still littered my mind.

"All right, when you're done, I'll take you over to Cal and
Beverly's."

I quickly finished the drink. Since Jamie had already paid for
our order, Mel and I left. He was a nice gentleman. He drove us two
miles to Cal and Beverly's home where he led me to their front door
and rang the doorbell.

A woman, also about Mom's age, opened the door and greeted
us with a warm smile. "Hi! Welcome! You must be Denise!" Mel
winked. The hostess continued, "I'm Beverly. My husband, Cal, is
working tonight. Come on in!"

"I'll be heading home, Bev," stated Mel as he turned to leave.
"Great meeting you!" he flashed another heartwarming smile. These
seemed like good, down to earth, country people. My shoulders
relaxed.

Beverly graciously stated, "Are you hungry? I made some brown-
ies." She extended a plate.

"Thank you!" I timidly replied. Inwardly my mind screamed.
I'm starved!

After I gobbled down the chocolaty goodness, Beverly softly
said, "You look exhausted. Would you like to go on to bed?"

"Yes, if you don't mind."

"No problem. Your bedroom is down the hall. Just follow me. Here, I'll take your bags."

My head soon was caressed by a soft pillow in the elegantly decorated bedroom. I smiled as I dozed off.

I woke up early without the use of an alarm clock. My stomach rumbled as the scent of bacon cooking wafted into my bedroom. I hurriedly dressed and applied my makeup. "Good morning!" Beverly greeted as I entered the kitchen. "I'm making bacon, scrambled eggs, and toast. There's coffee in the pot if you want some. Just have a seat at the table. Breakfast will be ready soon."

I felt like a princess. After eating the feast, I dabbed the corners of my lips. "Breakfast was delicious. Thank you!" I politely said.

"It is my pleasure. What are your plans for today?"

"I'm not sure. I don't even know what time Jamie wakes up!"

"I think he usually sleeps in, but I doubt he will today!" Beverly exclaimed. "We can move into the living room where we'll be more comfortable while we visit."

Jamie arrived within two hours. "I thought I could show you the sheriff's department!" Jamie sat down and devoured breakfast. "Bev, I'll have her back by bedtime!"

We rode Jamie's motorcycle downtown. I received a "grand tour" of the department. "Let's just leave the bike here. We can walk the rest of the way." We leisurely strolled through the downtown area. We stopped in each store as Jamie introduced me to store owners.

The day passed quickly. "Tomorrow we'll go swimming. I'll pick you up at nine!" Jamie declared before kissing me goodnight.

My second day was as starry as the first. We swam, ate a picnic lunch, went to the movie theater, and ate dinner at a pizza place.

I had to leave the next morning to be back at work on Tuesday. The bus ride back to Colorado Springs seemed even longer than the one to see Jamie. Dad and Mom picked me up at the bus depot. "Did you have a good time?" Dad asked.

"Yes! He showed me the entire town, introduced me to shop owners, coworkers, and his landlord. They were who I stayed with,

Cal and Beverly Dyrness. You'd really like them! We went swimming and to a movie! The bus moved as slow as a snail!"

Mom, Dad, and I chatted all the way home. I couldn't wait to sleep in my own bed! I was exhausted!

Jamie and I continued writing and making bi-monthly phone calls between his monthly visits. Time dragged on. We eagerly anticipated the start of our new life. My job at Colorado Interstate Gas kept me busy during the week. Working kept my mind from dwelling too much on our upcoming wedding.

*****

During a weekend phone conversation Jamie said, "I found an apartment! Cal and Beverly own it and just remodeled it! I can't wait for you to see it!"

"Great! I'm sure if Beverly had a hand in the remodel, it's perfect!"

A few nights later, as Dad, Mom, and I ate dinner, Dad asked, "How'd you like to go see your future home? I could drive you over Saturday. We'll check out your apartment, have lunch with Jamie, and then head home."

"Really? I'd love it! I'll call Jamie and let him know!"

The next weekend Dad and I visited during the drive. Since Jamie was working, his landlord, Beverly, let us into the apartment. *The place wasn't quite what I expected. Jamie told me it was recently remodeled. Remodeled? Huh.*

I expected new drywall, paint, carpet, up-to-date appliances. Instead, I saw a recently renovated pottery shop turned furnished apartment. The living room was barely big enough to accommodate an older couch, chair, gun cabinet, and a console TV. There was a small full closet with no door. Only a curtain separated it from the rest of the living room.

The kitchen was tiny. I opened the cabinets. Their contents revealed an interesting mix: salt, pepper, garlic, and cayenne pepper, fishing supplies, and a gun cleaning kit. There were only two things held in place with straight pins on the walls in the entire apartment—a calendar and a pocket watch.

The bedroom had no door. It was only big enough to hold a full-sized bed and a chest of drawers. The tiny closet barely held Jamie's uniforms. *Where would I put my clothes?* I gulped. *My current bedroom at Mom and Dad's was as big as this entire apartment!*

Dad's encouraging voice gently interrupted my thoughts. "This looks very homey." I forced a weak smile.

Jamie was only able to break free from work for a few minutes. Dad and I toured the town, visited with Beverly, and then left.

*****

The next time Jamie came to visit me the following month. I greeted him with a kiss. "I've missed you so much! Couldn't wait for you to get here! We need to pin down our ideas for our wedding! Hope ya don't mind, but I picked out a tux for you. What colors should we wear? I was thinking baby blue for you and your groomsmen and the bridesmaids. What kind of flowers do you want? Roses? Lilies? What about the cake? White or chocolate? Buttercream or traditional frosting?" I excitedly rattled off questions.

Jamie smiled as I finally inhaled. "I don't care about any of that stuff. I'll leave that up to you." *Good! That'll allow me, Mom and my friends to plan the wedding!* Several of Mom's friends volunteered to help. A close friend's mom planned to make our flower arrangements out of blue and white silk roses. Several women told Mom they'd serve refreshments; my music pastor, Terry Adams, said he'd sing. My parents rented the men's tuxedos from the Air Force Academy. *Should I mention to Jamie that they had ruffled shirts? Nah, he told me to plan everything. Besides, that's the latest trend and they'll match my bridesmaid's dresses perfectly.* Mom drove me to a nearby cake decorator where I chose the frosting, cake topper, and design. Mom and Dad paid for a professional wedding photographer.

Jamie and I went to my pastor, Grant, for marriage counseling during his next visit. I didn't realize that Jamie was like a little brother

34

to my pastor. As we entered Grant's office, he slapped Jamie's forehead with the heel of his right hand and then shouted, "Be healed!" The two broke into boisterous laughter and hugged. "Come on in and sit down! So you're finally getting married?" Jamie flashed a broad smile, "Yep!" That was the extent of our "marriage counseling."

Jamie and I continued writing. He called twice a month and visited once monthly. Four long months later, the day finally came!

Jamie warned me after our rehearsal dinner, "We've got to be sure we hide my Bronco! My friends will be at the wedding and I know they'll mess with it! I don't want them getting their hands on it. I'd hate to have anything on it so people know we're headed to our honeymoon!"

"What should we do?"

"Do you have anyone we can trust? Some place we can put it?"

"Yeah, I know just the place. Your...our car will be safe! I'll give you the address. Your best man can leave it there before you come to the church."

"Perfect!"

To my family's surprise, I slept in the morning of our wedding. After showering and packing a small bag, I pulled on my jeans and jumped in my parents' extra car. Leisurely I drove to the church. Dad and Mom were already there setting things up.

I carried a few things inside and then returned to my car where I grabbed a few more items. "Aren't you the bride?" inquired the surprised cake decorator as I reentered the church.

I replied with a wide smile, "Yep!"

Glancing to my right, I saw Jamie and his college friend, Michael. *Oops! It was bad luck for him to see me before the wedding!* I quickly went into the changing room, slipped off my everyday clothes and put on my wedding gown. It was a perfect fit. My bridesmaids, Cindy, my sister, and Suzanne, looked beautiful in their dresses. Butterflies fluttered in my stomach. I nervously waited for the pianist's music to begin. Can't believe I was minutes away from being married! I glanced at the clock again then again. The minute hand had barely moved. *Okay. Breathe, breathe, and relax your shoulders. Better check my watch. Maybe that clock's broken.* I lifted my gown's sleeve. *No. It wasn't broken! It was past time for the wedding to begin. Suzanne and Cindy should've both walked down the aisle by now!* What was going on? Finally, the anxious thoughts escaped my mouth, "What's the hold up? Why're we starting late?"

"I don't know. Want me to go check?" Cindy inquired.

I hope he didn't "stand me up." Emotionally deflated, I weakly responded, "Yeah, if you don't mind."

Several minutes later she returned. "Jamie and his best man aren't here!"

"What? I saw them not thirty minutes ago!" My stomach lurched. Shocked, I sat down on a nearby chair nervously tapping my foot. *My worst nightmare is happening! I'm being left at the altar without the groom!*

Finally, Dad poked his head in the door. "You ready?" he quietly asked.

Still panicked, I asked, "Is Jamie here?"

"Yes." Dad smiled as he gently replied. His calm voice reassured me. The pianist began playing. Suzanne exited the room. My wedding was underway!

Cindy left next, turning she gave me a reassuring smile. Dad gingerly placed his hand behind my back. Leaning over, he gently kissed my cheek. "I'm proud of you. I love you," he whispered. I slipped my arm through his as the wedding march began. I gulped, inhaled, and nodded toward Dad. I took the first step into the sanctuary. Everyone stood. Although the room was crowded, my eyes were only on Jamie's.

The wedding went beautifully. Although Jamie's brothers weren't able to come, his sister-in-law, Sandy, attended as well as my family. My paternal grandmother, Irene, and a few aunts and uncles came all the way from Oklahoma. Grandma brought small, netted bags full of rice she'd lovingly tied with pale blue bows.

We knelt as the pastor prayed. My choir director sang. Then we said our vows. In the blink of an eye, we were pronounced "man and wife."

Jamie politely fed me my piece of cake. With gratitude and excitement, we opened our bounty of gifts. As we left, attendees opened the bags of rice Grandma Irene made and wholeheartedly showered us with the contents.

A friend drove Jamie and I to our hidden car. As we entered my friend's long secluded driveway, we were greeted by fifteen or twenty friends, all laughing hysterically. Jamie erupted, "How'd they find my car?" He jumped out of the car and chased the marauders. "I'll get you for this!" Men scattered in every direction. Jamie began ripping signs off our car. I shyly approached, "Baby, can't we leave a few? We only get married once." Shrugging, he leaned toward me for a kiss. To Jamie's chagrin and my delight, several drivers gave us grins and "thumbs up" on our way to the hotel.

As we drove, I asked, "Why were you late for our wedding?"

Jamie nonchalantly shrugged. "Oh, I'm sorry about that! I got nervous waiting so Michael and I went and got some ice cream."

Maybe I should have been upset, but I wasn't. *It's my wedding day. Everything is perfect! This man, the man I love, is my husband!*

My roots strengthened as limbs branched out.
God gently nurtured His sapling.

5

Two nights after our honeymoon, Jamie was involved in a fight at work. He called it an "altercation." When he opened our door, I immediately noticed his clothes were covered in blood. "Baby, are you okay? What happened? What do you need me to do?"

"I'm fine, just got in a scuffle at work with a drunk. Most of the blood's the perp's. I'll change clothes. Would you get the blood and grease out of my uniform? Just soak the bloody areas in cold water. I have Goop under the sink for the grease. The dry cleaner will get the rest of the dirt out. I'd have them get the other junk off the uniform but that'd cost extra."

I grabbed the bloody pants with trembling hands. *Breathe, breathe, swallow, and breathe! Don't throw up! I could do this.* The scenario repeated itself two nights later.

The next week, Jamie bolted through our apartment door mid-shift. He breathlessly shouted, "Don't let anyone in! There's been a rape a block from here! We're still looking for the man!" Immediately, he slammed the door. After he left, I sat terrified, curled into a tight ball. I felt totally alone. *I wish he hadn't stopped in. I wouldn't have let anyone in… I don't think I would…maybe it is good he warned me.* I had never slept alone in a house before our marriage. I remained riveted to the couch until Jamie came home.

This was my first exposure to violence. Growing up I was naively innocent, rarely watching the news or reading newspapers. *Now I saw the dangerous reality of Jamie's job. I realized that any day could be our last. I placed Jamie into God's hands. Help us appreciate every minute we have together!*

As life gradually settled down, we adopted a daily routine. Around 11:00 a.m., Wednesdays through Sundays, Jamie and I meandered the downtown area of Glenwood Springs. We stopped in every shop and chatted with the owners.

Jamie knew each by name. "Hey, Tom! How's business today? Got any specials I can't live without?" Jamie ended every conversation with laughter, a hug, and a pat on the owner's back. Some of the men he considered as close as family. Jamie ended their pat with a three second neck massage.

I loved how he was so friendly and down to earth with people. My shoulders straightened with pride. I wondered how this charismatic man loved simple me.

To get a brief respite from the summer heat, we perused our local grocery store. Our gait slowed through the frozen food section. Afterward, we leisurely cruised the streets on Jamie's motorcycle. The scent of grilling burgers at the drive-through hamburger stand wafted through the warm air. Once a month, our budget permitted us to give in to the temptation.

Jamie proclaimed, "Man, I can't drive by this place another day without stopping! Let's splurge and get ourselves a burger!"

We always returned to our apartment by one thirty. Then Jamie dressed for work and left for his three-to-eleven shift. *Lord, be with him!*

Summer's heat raged on well into September. We only had two windows in our apartment. Both were on the west side making a breeze impossible. Jamie tied a fan in front of the living room window to force some air to move. One evening after he left for work, I got ready for bed in true newlywed fashion. I put on a sexy negligee then snuggled onto our couch waiting for my hubby's shift to end. Suddenly, the hair on the back of my neck stood up. I felt someone watching me! My gaze shot to the window. I saw a man's face peering at me through the fan! I was too scared to move off the couch and didn't know anyone's phone number to call for help! Shoot! I didn't even know the sheriff's department's number! (The 911 calling system hadn't yet been created.)

I froze in place, crying and praying until Jamie came home hours later. I leaped up and threw myself into his arms. My quivering voice eked out, "Someone was looking at me through our fan! I didn't know any phone numbers to call for help!"

Through gritted teeth he stated, "I'm so sorry, baby! I bet it was George!"

"Who's George?"

"He's a Peeping Tom who lives nearby. He was arrested for peering in windows a few weeks ago." I gulped and clung to Jamie tighter. Jamie grabbed a piece of paper jotting as he spoke. "Here are phone numbers for the sheriff's department, Cal and Beverly, and Mel. I want you to be able to defend yourself. We're going to the firing range. I'm going to teach you how to shoot."

Jamie followed through with his proclamation; my classes began the next day. "Have a seat, Gorgeous. I'm gonna make an Annie Oakley out of you!" He unloaded his gun. "Okay, there are no bullets in here. It's not dangerous. Anytime you pick up a gun, check to see if it is loaded. Treat every gun like it's loaded until you check. This is how to check this gun."

This can't be much different than the BB gun I shot as a kid. I can do this!

He patiently taught me the uses and names of every part of the weapon. Then he handed the empty weapon to me. The steel was colder than I expected. It wasn't difficult to pull the trigger.

"Pull the trigger a few times so you know how it feels. Good. Good. Now aim at the target. Use the sight to look down the barrel. Good. Now keep it in place and pull the trigger again. Good. Try this gun now. Yep. It fits your hand better. Do it several more times. Good. You did great! Do you have any questions?"

Blushing, I asked, "Yeah, can this student kiss the instructor?"

He consented!

Later that week Jamie drove me to the local shooting range. He reminded me of the proper way to stand. He calmly instructed,

"First, we'll put our ear protection on. Guns are pretty noisy. I'm starting you off with a .22 caliber. They have less kick. Once you're comfortable with that, you'll shoot my .38."

"Okay." I carefully reached for the weapon. I hoped I wouldn't embarrass myself!

Jamie's hand gently lay atop mine. "That's right. Don't be nervous. I'm right here with you." He removed his hand and stepped back. "Inhale, slowly exhale. Shoot whenever you're ready."

Thank You, Lord for my patient protective husband!

*****

Little by little I learned more about Jamie's job. One morning Jamie mentioned, "I remember locking myself out of the cruiser one night!" His head went back as he let out unrelenting laughter. "So I had to ask the man I was about to give a ticket to for a ride to the sheriff's department!" More laughter.

"What'd ya mean? Why couldn't you just call for help on your radio?"

"Call for help? Yeah, that'd be great, but my radio is in the car!" More laughter.

"You only have one radio? The one mounted to your dashboard?"

"Yeah, I couldn't give a guy a ticket and then ask for a ride!" Jamie chortled uncontrollably!

I forced a smile. *I had no idea how on his own he is! Lord, protect him!*

"Yeah, my nearest backup officer is often thirty minutes away."

I hugged him closely as I gulped.

Twice that year dispatch called me. A concerned woman's voice questioned, "Have you heard from Jamie?"

"No."

I thought that was your job!

"Oh. Okay, never mind."

"No! I can't 'never mind.' What's going on?"

"Well, it's probably nothing," her tone suddenly became very official. "We've just lost contact with him. He was chasing some bank robbers. Talk to you later. Bye."

My mind whirled. *What if he caught up to them and has been shot!* I called my parents. "Mom, would you and Dad please pray for Jamie? A dispatcher just called me. She said Jamie was chasing bank robbers and they lost contact with him!"

"Sure, honey. Let's pray right now. Lord, You know where Jamie is. Protect and keep him safe. Wrap your peace around both him and Denise. Amen. Let us know when you hear something."

"Okay. Love you. Bye!" I hung up, knelt repeating most of Mom's prayer, "Lord please keep Jamie safe! Be with him. Protect him!"

Eleven-thirty, midnight, one, two… *Oh! I hear a car driving up! It's him!*

As soon as our front door opened, I tightly hugged my man!

Dispatch called again a few months later. "Do you have your police scanner on?"

"No. We don't have one."

"Oh. Um, never mind."

"What's happening?"

"Well…um…nothing…"

"Please just tell me!"

"Can't! Sorry to bother you." Click. *Great! She hung up.* Immediately, I fell to my knees. Lord, here we go again! Please protect Jamie! I'm glad You know what's going on, but I'm just plain scared! Please be with Jamie!

I got up and called my parents. "Mom, it's me. Please pray for Jamie. Don't know what's going on but dispatch just called. He's in some kind of danger."

"Okay, honey. We'll be praying! Love you!"

I wiped my tears and breathed a sigh of relief when Jamie got home the next morning. *Thank You, God, for protecting him!*

After Christmas, our trailer park and apartment managers moved out of town. Jamie and I applied for and received their position. We immediately moved into the manager's quarters.

We felt as though we were living in the lap of luxury! *Goodbye, five-hundred-square-foot apartment. Hello, double-wide trailer! I have two bathtubs! Goodbye, laundromat! I have my own washer and dryer!*

I loved keeping the park's account books. Jamie did well handling people's problems and questions. Our tenants were either senior citizens, living in the trailers or young single residents in the apartments. A few of the elderly "adopted" us. We visited them often.

It wasn't long before I learned that any citizen could have a police scanner. One day I asked, "I've heard that other people have police scanners in their homes. Can we get one so I know what's happening?"

"No. Things always sound worse on the radio than they really are," Jamie answered. *That makes sense to me.* I didn't ask again.

Jamie's little brother, Jeff, called one Saturday. "Hi, Jeff! How ya doing…? What…? When…? Awesome! Why don't you come to Glenwood? I'll start asking around to see if anyone needs an employee!"

As he hung the phone up, I asked, "What's up?"

"Jeff's out of the navy! He and Sandy are going to move here!" He reached over and gave me a bear hug.

I barely knew her but she seemed nice! Maybe she'd give me company while Jamie was at work! Jeff and Sandy arrived a few days later. They moved into our first apartment. Jeff got a job; Sandy was hired by a local craft store. Since Jeff had been in the navy throughout their entire marriage, they enjoyed their time alone together.

So much for company while Jamie works! Jeff and Sandy only come over on Jamie's days off. So much for me having any time alone with Jamie! The three of them told stories from their shared past. *My past wasn't with them! I've been part of Jamie's life less than a year!* I permitted envy and resentment to bore itself into my spirit.

44

Before our originally planned date, I had morning sickness. Our doctor confirmed our suspicions, "You're pregnant." We were so poor we couldn't afford maternity clothes or items for our coming child. It seemed as though everything we owned broke, one thing after another: our car, my glasses, our radio, our television.

Jamie and I occasionally got together with two other young couples we met at church. After hearing about some of our financial struggles, one of Jamie's friends spoke to him. "Jamie, you've tried your way with finances since the beginning of your marriage. Now, why don't you try God's way for three months? God asks His children to give a tithe, 10 percent of their income, to Him. Why don't you try it? If God doesn't prove Himself faithful in providing, go back to doing things your way. But if God is faithful, depend on Him from now on."

Jamie doubtfully agreed, "Okay, I'll try things 'God's way' for three months." He expected debt collectors to call within two months. They didn't need to call us; God graciously blessed our small income.

A few months later, we received a package from my former pastor and his wife. It was a huge box—approximately three feet long by three feet wide by two feet deep. I enthusiastically opened the cardboard. *Look at all these baby boy clothes! I've never seen any this cute!* "Jamie, we're having a boy! God provided all his clothes!"

A few months later, our son was born. We named him John, gift of God. I was released from the hospital two days later. I'd never experienced anything like the love I had for this tiny baby! I never tired of looking into his eyes and watching his expressions and movements! He was quite a gift! He gave me company in the evenings while Jamie worked!

Jeff and Sandy, two of John's first visitors, shared our excitement. Because their jobs didn't pan out in the expensive community, they moved away within a couple of months.

When John was several months old, Jamie got called out in the middle of the night. I decided to feed John since I was already awake. Soon after eating, John threw up all over me. My gown was totally soaked! I quietly laid him in his crib, being careful not to wake him.

After I slipped into our master bathroom, I removed my soiled clothes. Suddenly, a man's deep voice said, "Hello" through the open window. My blood drained to my feet. I crumpled to the floor. *Lord, help!*

I threw on my clothes and crawled out to John's room. After scooping him up, I snaked my way back to my bedroom, carefully cradling my baby. I stayed hidden at the end of my bed, John in one hand, gun in the other, until Jamie got home.

Was the call falsified? Did this guy know Jamie from work? Did he figure out where Jamie lives? Was he watching to see when Jamie's patrol car rolled away from our house? Did he call the police, report a fictitious crime, watch Jamie leave? Did he know I'm alone? Like a hunter baited his game, every evil imaginable thought the enemy got me to bite hung in my mind.

After that, staying alone was torturous for me. *I was too terrified to open a window after Jamie leaves for work.* Every afternoon I locked the door, closed all windows, and kept John close to me. We sweltered until our protector got off work around 3:00 a.m. the next morning.

I called dispatch several times a week, "I'm scared. Please send Jamie to check on me."

One morning Jamie commented, "Denise, after you call, the dispatchers and other deputies laugh and tease me all night! We need to come up with a different solution."

Finally, I came up with an idea, When I was afraid, I called dispatch and left a message for Jamie to get milk on his way home.

Jamie decided it was a wonderful solution. When he got the message, he knew I was afraid and checked on me when he could break free. That stopped his coworker's taunts.

A few months later, John had to have hernia surgery. He was only eleven months old. *Lord, I hated that Jamie couldn't take any time off of work!* The hospital didn't have a children's ward or pediatric nurses, so John was in a regular room!

One morning, as I walked to his room, I passed a nurse's desk. One nurse leaned over to another and loudly whispered, "That screaming brat's mom is finally back!"

I plodded to his hospital room with heavy shoulders. John's medical needs fell solely on my shoulders. *Oh, no! I hear him crying all the way down this sterile hall!* Tears welled up in my eyes. I scurried down the long harshly lit hallway to John's room. I stroked his head and sang to him. He calmed down briefly before starting up again. He cried for what seemed like hours. *I can't handle this! I need a few minutes to be alone!* Tears ran down my cheeks. I quickly left the hospital, went to the car, and let myself inside. Collapsing, I angrily cried out to God. "Why can't anyone be here with me to help me? Why do I have to go through this alone?"

Suddenly, I heard a firm voice, not audibly, but in my spirit. "I could have had everyone be here for you, but I wanted you to learn to depend on Me alone. I'm here for you."

Peace and strength engulfed me. *Wow! Okay, we'll do this together.* I straightened my back, gathered my things, and marched back to John's room. I held my head high. I was accompanied by my all-powerful Heavenly Father!

My trunk and branches were bolstered
as the Forester taught me to depend on Him.

6

One morning, our phone rang as Jamie and I were eating breakfast. I answered, "Hello."

"Hi, Denise," I smiled, recognizing my sister's voice. "Guess what! Jeff's tour of duty is up in the air force! He's looking for a job in law enforcement in Colorado soon. We wonder if Jamie could help him!"

"Awesome! I'm sure he will! Give me the dates Jeff will be here." Yeah! My sister might get to move back close to me!

Jeff flew in several weeks later. Jamie picked him up at the Denver airport and drove him to Glenwood Springs. "I've got an appointment set up for you tomorrow with the sheriff."

"Thank you. Fill me in on the department." The two conversed easily.

Jeff left the next day to apply at other locations. He was hired by one on the eastern plains. Eighteen months later Jeff called, "Jamie's boss called and offered me a job! I'll be working with Jamie! We're heading your way in two weeks! Cindy, Jeff and their fourteen-month-old daughter moved in with us till they could find a house.

I loved that Cindy, Jeff, and their daughter, Jessica, lived with us. Their daughter was only four months older than John. Our husbands worked the same shift, so Cindy and I had plenty of time to talk and laugh. A couple of weeks later, they found a place to buy only thirty minutes away from us.

Thank You, Lord! I'm happy Cindy's close again but I wish she lived where we didn't have to pay long-distance rates on our phone calls! We'll only be able to afford to talk once a month.

The trailer court we managed was an "adult only" community. John was now a year old. Jamie and I knew we needed to move. He brought up the topic one morning, "There's no use denying it. We've got to find a different place to live. I've been keeping my eyes open, but man! Rents skyrocketed! I wonder if we wouldn't be better buying something."

"Do you really think we could?" *Having our own place would be a dream come true!*

We studied our budget. Jamie called our bank. "What's the current interest rate for a loan? Mm-hmm. It'll be a home loan. Yes, we're first-time home buyers. Okay, thank you for your help."

I watched Jamie's expression go from excitement to concern. "What'd they say?"

"The current rate is 12.5 percent! We're going to have to find a place as inexpensive as possible."

After searching for a couple months, we found a small condominium thirty minutes from Glenwood Springs. *We'd be twenty minutes from Cindy and Jeff and phone calls won't be long distance! I could call whenever I want for free!*

We moved from our trailer court manager position to our own home! We were thrilled as we settled into the new place. *We weren't renters any longer!*

Both exhausted, we only had the time and energy to get John's crib put up. Jamie and I slept on the living room floor. *We'd fill our waterbed the next day.*

I slept soundly all night. When I woke up, Jamie was sitting at our kitchen table. I smelled the coffee brewing. I stood and stretched. Jamie smiled, "Morning Baby. Did you sleep good in our new home?"

"Sure did! How long you been up?"

"Oh, I don't know. Not too long."

I sat down in the chair next to his. *He didn't look like he slept much.* "Is everything okay?"

"Yeah. I had a strange dream. Actually, I'm not even sure it was a dream."

"What was it about?"

"Well, like I said, I think it was a dream, but it was more real than any dream I've ever had. It was strange. I feel weird saying this but I almost wonder if it was a vision."

"Okay? Tell me about it."

"Well, it was short but I can't get it out of my mind. I stood in front of hundreds of people, and I was preaching."

"Preaching?"

"Yeah, preaching. Then it was over. Nothing else but I can't get it out of my mind."

"Do you want to pray about it with me?"

"Sure." We held hands, then bowed our heads. "Lord, I don't understand why my dream made me feel the way I feel this morning. I ask you to show me what my dream meant. Amen."

As we lifted our heads, my shoulders relaxed. I knew this moment was implanted deep in my heart and would stay in my mind forever.

"Up! Up!" John called us to get him out of his crib. He was ready for breakfast. Today would be full. We tried to get as much unpacked as possible during Jamie's second day off.

The two-bedroom condominium was perfect. It was so fun decorating my own place!

A week later, Jamie answered our phone when it rang, "Hello, hi, Steve! Where are you? Sure! We're just down the street on the left. See you soon!"

"What's up?"

"We're going to have our first company! Steve and Torie are at the post office. They drove to town to see our place! They'll be here any minute!"

Our first visitors—friends from Glenwood! Any minute! Yikes! Everything's a mess! I quickly threw things into the nearest closets.

Before we caught our breath, a knock sounded on the door. Jamie warmly greeted the young couple, "Come in! Come in! Let me give you the grand tour!"

We proudly escorted them from room to room. To my horror, Jamie opened every closet! *Ugh! Why are you showing them the closets? They're closets for Pete's sake!* Somehow, I swallowed my pride and chuckled. Jamie and the couple howled with laughter.

Soon, Jamie learned the sheriff's department was testing for a detective position. Immediately he applied for, was accepted, and was transferred to the job. *He's working days, has weekends off, and has a department car to drive home. Life is so good!* This job provided mental challenges for Jamie, as well as a small pay raise.

Weekly we went to church together for the first time since getting married. Our small country church was only eight miles from our condominium. *I can't believe I even get to be part of my sister's church. The people are friendly and don't put on airs. They even have a deaf ministry! I've always wanted to continue signing.* The pastor's wife taught a sign language class for anyone interested on Sunday evenings. Cindy and I registered for the course. Within a year, we were helping interpret the songs for the Sunday morning service. *God enabled our signing to exceed our training.*

A few months later, the church was informed that the pastor and his family were moving. Cindy and I were asked to step in and sign for the entire Sunday morning service. We took turns alternating interpreting the singing and preaching. Another woman who also knew sign language joined our efforts, which made a threefold signing team.

*****

My sister gave birth to her second child in January. A few days later I hinted, "Babe, we always agreed it would be good to have our kids two and a half to three years apart."

Without looking up from his task, Jamie replied, "Yeah."

"Well, John will be two in March. Think I should stop using birth control?"

"Sounds good to me! It'll probably take several months before you get pregnant anyway."

A week later, my doctor confirmed my suspicion. *I felt just like this when I was pregnant with John.*

My hormones keep me on an unending downhill emotional trajectory! I 'm angry, depressed, and want everyone around me to feel my misery! I didn't feel like this last time.

Cramping began four months later. One evening, I silently watched the clock. "Jamie, I hate to say this, but I've been having contractions for the last forty-five minutes."

"Are you sure?"

I nodded.

"Let me know when you have another one."

"Okay." He didn't have to wait long. "Now."

Jamie placed his hand on my stomach. "Feels pretty strong."

"Yeah."

"I'm timing how far apart they are." We both watched my enlarged belly. "Wow! Eight minutes!"

"That's about what I thought."

"I'll call someone to watch John. Grab your things and get in the car. I'm taking you to the hospital." We dropped our boy off with church friends. Jamie rushed me to the hospital twenty minutes away.

"Baby, can you walk in by yourself or do I need to walk you in?"

"I'll meet you inside, thanks."

After registering, a nurse put a belt connected to a machine around me. "This will measure your contractions. Push this button if you need anything."

Guess it's not urgent since no one's really keeping an eye on me. Several hours later, a doctor appeared. "I don't believe you're in full labor. Follow up with your OB-GYN."

Jamie carefully drove me home and then went to complete his swing shift at work. The next day he drove us to my doctor's office.

After examining me, my physician declared, "I'm concerned about the baby. I'm limiting your activity. Don't lift anything over ten pounds, walk long distances, or do heavy work."

He's got to be kidding! John weighs at least twenty pounds!

The contractions grew in intensity throughout June. At my next checkup, my physician sternly instructed, "You're restricted to absolute bed rest. No lifting. No work."

Great, now I can't do anything! Take care of John, cook, clean. I'm a prisoner in my own body!

My parents drove the five-hour trip to get John the next day. They took him to their home. Jamie's folks agreed to take turns watching him every other week.

I was glad they could help, but I missed my boy!

The contractions continued. Jamie drove me to the ER throughout July. My doctor put me on medication hoping to stop the contractions.

This chemical's making me feel crazy! Every tiny noise causes my skin to crawl! I'm lonely but can't stand to be around people!

I explained my feelings to my OB at my next appointment. He prescribed a medication to calm me. Now, every evening, Jamie came home to a grouchy wife who'd lain in bed all day, too exhausted to get up, too irritable to think about anyone but herself. Orders immediately erupted from my mouth, "Wipe your feet! Pick up your dirty laundry! Did you get groceries on your way home?"

I hated being unable to control my mind or my mouth. I didn't know which of us was more miserable, Jamie or me.

Days crept by as if in slow motion. Our only TV was in the living room; the only radio stations we received were country music. Everyone I knew worked. *I can't stand being home alone! I've gotta get out of the house!* That evening, I confronted Jamie, "I'm going to church with you this Sunday."

"You are? How're ya gonna do that?"

"I'm going to ride with you."

"But you're supposed to be on bed rest. You can't leave the house."

"I know, but one Sunday won't hurt. I'm going nuts. I need to get out in the world."

The following Sunday, I kept my word. My excitement blossomed with each passing mile. *Oh, we're almost there! I can't wait to see everyone!* Jamie interrupted my thought. "Think I'll stop and grab some gum."

"What? Now? We'll be late!"

"Nah, we'll be fine."

We've got five minutes before the pianist starts playing! I hate when Jamie thinks we're "on time" if we walk in as the service starts! These thoughts permeated until they bolted out of my mouth, "We do not have time to stop!"

"I'm stopping."

"If you stop, I'm getting out of the car! I'll walk to church!"

"Fine. Do what you want, but I'm stopping."

"Pull over!"

"Right here?"

"Yes!"

He complied. I burst out of the car and slammed the door. *That'll show him.* I stood with arms crossed watching him turn the car around. *He'll be back. In all the movies I've seen, the man always comes back and apologizes. Minutes passed. Where'd he go? Did he really just leave me? It's almost a half mile to the church! He wouldn't leave his pregnant wife; I'm supposed to be on bed rest!* Light drizzle fell. Panic sank into my mind. *He did leave me!* My shoulders slouched as I trudged toward the church. The enemy cast worst case scenarios into my mind. *What if he's left me forever? I'm going to be a single mother with two kids!* Tears poured as I walked the remaining distance to the church. *I don't want anyone to see me. I'll just slip in and grab my sister. Maybe she'll take me home.* Sniffling, I dried my tears before I entered the building.

An usher greeted me, "Denise! Are you okay?"

"Yeah, just need Cindy."

"I'll get her for you." He left me cowering at the entrance, walked down the aisle, and leaned down to whisper in my sister's ear. Her head whipped around. She grabbed her purse and joined me.

"Is everything okay?"

I shook my head. *Don't speak, I'll start crying and won't be able to stop!*

"Come on. I'll drive you home."

Tears flowed freely after getting into her car. On the way home, I recounted the whole ugly incident. "Thanks for not judging me. I feel really stupid. Jamie must've not watched the same movies I did!"

"Obviously not!" We both chuckled.

Once home, I slowly opened my front door. *Okay, girl, time to eat humble pie!* Stepping into our living room, I immediately saw Jamie sitting comfortably on our couch reading the paper. His gaze met mine as a corner of his lips curled up slightly.

That smirk said it all. He knew the meds were making me crazy, he understood, he forgave. United laughter erupted.

*****

The contractions were stronger and consistent in the pregnancy's seventh month. Jamie drove me to my next scheduled appointment. My physician instructed, "You need to be hospitalized so we can get the contractions under control. I want to put you on an IV medication. I'm admitting you into the hospital."

"I need to go home and get some things."

"No. Go straight to the hospital. Someone can bring anything you need later."

Jamie commented, "The doc's right. I'll get your stuff later."

Jamie drove me straight to the hospital. After checking in, I was assigned a room. A nurse entered within minutes and started an IV. "Because this medication is so strong, I'll be monitoring you."

I watched the medicine slowly drip into the IV line. Within minutes, my arm felt incredible squeezing pressure.

The pain's getting worse. I can't seem to breathe deeply.

"I'm having a hard time breathing."

"Okay. Let's sit your bed up." Seconds after she raised my bed, I passed out. My eyes opened to a roomful on concerned doctors. Oxygen tubes were in my nose.

Frightened, I weakly told a nurse, "Please, call my husband."

A doctor explained, "We want to try the medicine again but give you a smaller dose. It must have been too much medication for someone your size."

Another interjected, "I think she had a panic attack. We didn't give her anything that would cause her to pass out."

The first commented again, "Let's wait thirty minutes before starting the IV again." Half an hour later they reconvened in my room. "Okay, let's try this again."

"The room's getting dark and fuzzy."

A man bellowed, "Stop the IV!"

I lost consciousness. When I came to, I saw the same concerned faces. "Just keep her hospitalized. Watch her closely."

I started to cry a couple of days later as the contractions grew stronger and more frequent.

What's going on? Am I going to lose this baby?

A nurse slipped in quietly and asked, "May I pray for you?" She tenderly held my hand then voiced a short, peace-filled prayer. She exited as quickly and quietly as she'd arrived.

That was strange. I've never seen that woman in this tiny hospital before. Her prayer was exactly what I needed. Thank You, Lord. Was she an angel? I guess it really doesn't matter. I know whoever or whatever she was, You sent her.

Two weeks later, my OB doctor entered my room and announced, "Your baby is old enough now to survive when it's born. You're being discharged."

I telephoned Jamie, "Hi, Hon, I'm being discharged! I'm no longer on bed rest! Don't have to take those ugly meds anymore! Call our parents. Let's get our boy home!"

I smiled as I peered out our front window the following afternoon. "John will be here any minute! I can't wait!" Finally, my in-law's car pulled into our parking lot. "They're here! They're here!"

Terri carried John inside. He stood with his arms crossed by the front door. I slowly lowered myself down to the floor directly in front of him, opening my arms for a long-awaited hug. "John, I've missed you so much!" He smiled and ran to Jamie. My shoulders drooped. Jim, Terri, and Jamie broke into laughter. *It's not funny! He's my baby and won't even look at me!* He hugged me two days later. *Apparently, I was forgiven for "abandoning" him.* Jamie pushed John's stroller as I waddled beside him on daily family walks during the next month.

It's wonderful having our family together again!

Time crept forward.

One morning a couple of weeks later, Jamie announced, "Dad and Mom are coming over this weekend. Dad and I want to go hunting."

"What?" *Doesn't he know this baby's due anytime? Is he crazy?*

"We'll only be gone during the day. I'll be sure to be home at night. Mom will be here with you and John if anything happens."

"But…"

How can he leave after all we've gone through?

My cheeks flushed crimson.

"You'll be fine. I promise we'll be home every night."

"You better be home! If you miss this baby's birth, don't bother coming home!"

Jim and Terri came as they'd planned. The men left the next morning. Jamie tried to reassure me as he exited, "See you tonight!" Light drizzle fell as he closed the front door.

The mist turned to snow shortly after they left. My brow creased, "What if they don't make it home?"

Terri attempted to console me as she crocheted, "They'll be back."

The weather continued to worsen throughout the day. "This doesn't look good."

"It'll be fine."

It'll be fine? You've got to be kidding! Jamie better make it home or we won't be fine!

"Besides, if you go into labor and they're not here, I can go in with you. Sandy let me go in with her when Jesse was born. She's such an amazing mom! She did wonderfully!"

Hmph! Sandy's amazing. I was anything but amazing delivering John. Doubt I'll be any better this time! I want this baby's father with me!

Terry made delicious stew for dinner. Before scooping it up, she said, "Oh! I almost forgot! I brought a care package for you to take to the hospital!"

Straighten up. She's doing her best to be nice to me!

"Thank you! You didn't have to get me anything!" Excitedly I opened the basket containing a magazine, slippers, lip balm, and fingernail polish. "I love everything! Thank you!" The telephone rang as we finished eating.

"Hello?"

My brow furrowed as I heard Jamie's voice. I looked at Terri.

"Hi, babe."

"What's up?"

"You're not going to be happy…"

"What's up?"

"The rain and snow made the roads too slippery to come home tonight. We're going to spend the night at a friend's house. We'll head home as soon as the road clears tomorrow."

"You're kidding, right?"

"No, Hon, I'm sorry, but we really are stuck for the night."

I turned my back to Terri.

Lowering my voice, I grumbled, "You know what I told you. You better get here tomorrow! Good night."

"We'll be there tomorrow. Love you! Night." The men arrived the next afternoon—two days before my baby's due date.

After nine tortuous months, the day arrived. Jamie drove me to my obstetrician. After finishing my exam, the physician asked, "You ready to have this baby? It's your due date!"

"Yes, sir."

"I can induce your labor tonight. I'll meet you at the hospital around seven."

"Induce?"

"Yes, after all the medications you've taken to stop contractions, you'll never go into labor naturally."

That would've been nice to know last weekend!

Nine hours after labor was induced, the doctor proclaimed, "it's a girl!" Tears of joy trickled from mine and Jamie's eyes as my hubby tenderly kissed my forehead. That afternoon, I hold my precious child closely.

I know what I'll do; I'll polish her perfect fingernails! I tenderly opened Shannon's fist, gently releasing tiny fingers around the palm of my left hand. The pale pink fingernail polish went on quickly. Carefully I blew the polish dry. I repeated the process on the other hand. *There! They look so cute!*

My daughter slept soundly. I called the nursery, "Hi, this is Denise Royal. Please have someone come and take my baby back to the nursery. I need to get some sleep." I dozed off as soon as they left my room.

A sharp shout abruptly awoke me, "What have you done? You can't put fingernail polish on a newborn! We can't check her circulation! You have to remove it immediately!"

"I'm so sorry! I didn't know it'd be a problem," I shrugged. "I don't have any remover."

The nurse shook her head. "We'll have to search the entire hospital to find some!"

Whew! I didn't mean to make such a fuss! Lesson learned!

The hospital nursery's staff wouldn't keep Shannon with the other babies. Her cry was so loud she woke all the other infants! The nurses insisted she stay in my room as long as possible.

My daughter and I were released from the hospital on October 20, my twenty-second birthday. *What a precious gift. She's beautiful! I love her rosy, plump cheeks and mass of black hair!* I inhaled deeply. *Umm, her newborn smell makes me smile!*

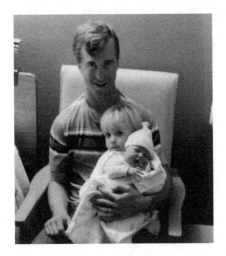

A week later I climbed out of bed and exclaimed, "I feel great! Let's have someone over for lunch this Sunday after church."

Surprise registered in Jamie's eyes. "I'm game if you're up to it!" he grinned.

He seems as relieved as I am to have my pre-pregnant self back!

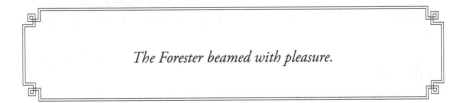

The Forester beamed with pleasure.

Shannon's so different from my easy-going John. His whisper quiet, lamblike-cry was barely audible when he needed me.

Our condominium neighbors heard all of Shannon's relentless squalling.

Nothing soothes her non-stop crying. That is...till her Dad walks in, picks her up, and holds her against his chest. Then, she's immediately quiet. My "precious" baby's almost two months old. Why isn't she like her brother? What am I doing wrong?

One evening, I restated the concern with my hubby, "Jamie, I don't know what to do with Shannon. She won't stop crying. I do everything I know to calm her. Nothing works. I'm at my wit's end!"

"She cries all day?"

"Yes, every day. I feed her, change her diapers, rock her, pace with her, but she won't stop crying!"

His forehead furrowed. "She doesn't cry after I get home."

"I know. I've noticed."

"I'm sorry, honey. I don't know what to tell you. I'm sure she'll do better with time."

A few days later, I walked into the living room to find John sitting on Shannon's stomach. "John! Get off your sister!"

Scowling, he obeyed. "Take her back!"

"John, she's your sister. We don't take her back. She's a part of our family now. We just love her."

Shannon let out a loud howl. John's hands clamped over his ears. I reached for my daughter. "Shh, it's okay. There, there, Mommy has you. Shh…John, I'll read you a book when Shannon quiets down." Screaming continued until she wore herself out and fell asleep.

Weeks morphed into months. Shannon's tearful, earsplitting fits gradually eased.

My mood, however, didn't lighten. Each day I became more despondent. By the time Shannon was six months old my depression reached a new depth.

I should be thrilled to be home, to have a baby girl. Instead, I just feel sad. I don't care if I get out of bed. I don't care about anything, Lord. I don't know what's wrong. Am I a complete failure? Help me feel like myself again!

Depression was my unrelenting antagonist; it drained every aspect of my life. My hormones gradually readjusted from pregnancy and delivery. One morning as I prayed, God nudged my heart, "Read your Bible. You'll be encouraged."

The kids clamored for my attention as I attempted to resume daily times with God.

Quiet time with God isn't quiet. The few verses I'm able to read each day remind me of a desert wasteland. My heart feels as though God's uncaring and distant. I rarely receive insight or direction from Him.

"Lord, I read and read your Word but I don't hear You speaking to me! I'm really frustrated!"

Silence.

Weeks later, I still pleaded. *God, please hear me! Please speak to me!*

Nothing.

Months passed. Daily, I asked. *Are you there? Do You hear?*

One day a soft voice whispered, "Denise, do you and Jamie spend time together only when you have something important to say? No, you just enjoy being together. I want you to spend time with Me even when it doesn't seem like I'm talking. I want you to spend time with Me. I want you to grow comfortable being with Me. When I do speak, you will hear Me!"

Okay, if I build my relationship with You, even through the dry times, when You do have something to tell me, I'll recognize Your voice. Wow! I get it! Thank You!

His words quieted my heart. The next day, I restarted my time in God's word with renewed respect, appreciation, and anticipation.

*****

Our family occasionally went to the local reservoir in the evenings. I packed a picnic dinner for us to eat. After our meal, John played with trucks in the dirt; Shannon lay on a blanket. Jamie and I fished from the quiet shore.

Other evenings, we went to church or friends' homes, had guests over for dinner, or just stayed home. Unable to afford cable TV, we only received a very grainy PBS station on our television. We nicknamed our kids our own personal entertainment centers.

*****

After work one day, Jamie mentioned, "You'll never believe who I heard from today."

"Who?"

"Susan."

"Susan? Who's she?"

"You know, I dated her before we met."

"What'd she want?"

"Nothing much, just mentioned that we probably have a couple of kids by now. She said that you're probably flabby, and that she's in great shape."

"Great. She sounds like trouble. I hope you never hear from her again."

"Don't know why I would."

Shannon's cries from the next room ended our conversation.

*****

Soon, after learning to crawl, Shannon was able to reach my houseplants.

"No, no, don't touch Mommy's plant." *I remember when John was several months past this age. I'd tap the back of his hand. Huge crocodile tears pooled in his eyes. End of lesson. He didn't do it a second time.*

Keeping her eyes on me, Shannon brushed the foliage with her hand.

I walked over and gently patted the back of her hand. "No, no." As I backed away, she took a death grip on the plant. Then she stripped an entire stalk.

"I said, 'No, no!'" Reaching down, I firmly swatted her hand. Shannon glared at me defiantly as she grasped and stripped the second.

This time her hind end received a strong thump.

This kid's stubborn!

Each day brought new battles of our wills. One Sunday I was informed by the church's nursery worker that Shannon bit another child. I waited until we arrived home to talk to her about it.

"Shannon, Miss Mary said you bit a little girl. Did you bite someone?"

Her face moved up and down. She responded in her own language, "Mrnph!"

"That's not nice. It hurts when you bite."

Insubordination shot from her eyes. "Mrnph!"

Oh my, the battle is on. I reached her arm, lifted it to my mouth, and gently bit.

Shannon's eyes remained locked with mine. Her eyes narrowed. She lifted her arm to her mouth and then bit until she drew blood.

Lord, what do I do? Do I pray over her, wait for her head to spin around? What do I do? The battle's over. I guess she won this one.

No matter what she did, I couldn't keep from smiling. *I can't tell if it's the gleam in her eyes, her cockiness, or that she's just flat adorable, but I can't keep from laughing!*

Shannon learned to walk at only twelve months. Her tiny feet required specially ordered hard-soled shoes. She went from tottering to running within weeks.

Great! Now I can start potty-training. John was so easy. He learned within a week. I just gave him an M&M every time he used the toilet. As bright as Shannon is, this'll be a piece of cake!

"Shannon, you get to have new panties! Here, I'll put them on you." The extra small training pants fit perfectly. "Now that you're a big girl, you get to use the potty. You'll get a special treat every time you pee in it. Let me know when you have to pee."

After a few accidents, she grasped the idea. One morning, she ran to me, "Uh-uh!" She grabbed my hand, led me to the restroom and climbed onto the commode. She let out two drops of urine then held out her hand.

"Good girl, I'm so proud of you! Here's your treat!" I handed her an M&M candy.

She flashed a triumphant smile before jumping down and pulling up her undies. I flushed the toilet.

She screamed, "Grrmp call myfer!"

"What'd I do wrong?"

"Grrmp myfer!"

"Do you want to flush the toilet?"

Her head bobbed.

"Okay, next time, you can flush."

She acknowledged victory with a grin.

Guess she told me!

Five minutes later I hear, "Uh-huh."

"You have to go again?"

Nodding resumed. She ran to the bathroom. Shannon was already sitting on the toilet when I entered the room. Two drops later, she held out her hand. Our eyes met. She cocked her head to one side and smiled. *She's a bright one. What worked for John isn't going to work for her. At this rate, we'll go through the whole bag of candy by bedtime.*

"I'll be right back with your treat." I returned with raisins.

"Grf me tuff grg!" she complained.

"You're a good girl and did a good job. You get two special raisins!"

"Grf greb."

"You get two very special raisins!"

Our eyes locked before she reluctantly accepted her prize.

Our 850-square-foot condominium felt small with two active kids. On nice days, I let the kids play on our front sidewalk. *How can I make sure they stay out of the gravel parking lot? I know! I'll take one shoe off each child's foot every day.* Strategically, I removed their other shoe the following day. *This'll keep their feet tender so they'll stay close to our front door.*

Jamie and I bought two inexpensive paint brushes. The next bright day, I gave each their new treasure. The three of us exited our home eagerly anticipating a new adventure. I set a small bucket of water on the railroad ties in our entryway.

"Kids, I need you to paint our house. Dip your brush in the pail like this, and then wipe it on the siding like this. Good. You're doing a great job!"

The wet brushes darkened the wooden siding. My students gleamed with pride over their accomplishments.

The two "painted" for almost fifteen minutes while I returned to my dirty dishes.

John's scream grabbed my attention, "Mom! Shannon dumped the water!"

So much for this keeping the kids busy!

Several weeks later, Jamie arrived home to find the kids alone in our living room. He called out, "Denise?"

I heard steps coming toward our bedroom. He gently knocked on the door and then tenderly asked, "Is everything okay?"

"No! The kids won't stay in their room! The only way I can get some peace and quiet is to lock myself in our room!"

"It's okay now, I'm home, babe."

God tenderly nurtured His young tree.
He gently staked me to keep me from becoming bent.
All I felt were seemingly cruel restraints,
Many days, I questioned His goodness.

8

My sister called a few weeks later, "I just read about an interpreting/tutoring job at a local elementary school working with a deaf child."

"Really? What'd the ad say?"

Cindy read the ad to me. After our conversation, I immediately called. "Hello. This is Denise Royal. Are you still looking for a deaf interpreter and tutor?"

"Yes. Please give me your name and phone number and someone will call you."

I received a phone call an hour later setting up an interview.

My hands trembled throughout the meeting. After a few days, I received a phone call. A pleasant-sounding male voice asked, "Mrs. Royal?"

"Yes."

"The school would love to hire you. Can you start Monday morning?"

"Absolutely! Thank you for the opportunity!" I gushed.

"Please be here at seven thirty so you can fill out some paperwork and meet your boss. You will be needed Monday through Friday from eight to noon. The student you'll be working with is a third-grade girl. Her name is Cassy."

Before I left for work each day, I cleaned the house and prepared dinner, then took the kids to their baby sitter.

The meager bit of money helped a little with our budget. I had weekends, holidays, and the summer off.

What a perfect job! Thank You, Lord! I love this! The young girl I work with is so sweet!

Now, the kids kept me laughing most of the time. However, one day after I picked them up from day care, I buckled them into their seats and headed home. As I turned the car onto the highway, fighting between the two began immediately. John screamed first, "Give me back my book!"

Then Shannon screamed, "Mnmph!"

Back and forth they volleyed.

"What's going on?" I interrupted.

"She's taking my book!" John angrily declared.

"Shannon, give John his book."

More screaming.

"Now what?"

"Now I have the book, and she wants it!"

"If you two don't stop fighting, I'm going to pull over and spank you both!"

More fighting. More screaming. "Okay. That's it." I pulled the car onto the side of the road, unbuckled, and turned around.

"John, I told you to give her the book!"

"I did, Mom! It's a pretend book!"

Flabbergasted I re-buckled.

My forehead rested for a few seconds on the steering wheel.

They're working together to steal my sanity.

*****

Our church hired a new pastor shortly after our last one moved. God worked mightily. Many people asked Jesus into their lives. Jamie and I rapidly matured spiritually.

Jamie dealt with work's stress pretty well most of the time. That is, until a man was executed at a gas station a few miles from our house. Then, he worked around the clock. He couldn't take a day off until the case was resolved. Jamie's church attendance became sporadic.

When the department was unable to solve the murder, Jamie hit a wall mentally, physically, and emotionally. As other crime's cases piled up, the murder was buried under other paperwork. The file may have been out of sight, but never left his mind. Exhausted and discouraged, Jamie walked into our kitchen one morning and announced, "I'm going to apply for a job at the Colorado Springs Police Department."

"What?" I asked glancing up from the dishes I was rinsing.

"Well, the economy's so bad here. Since Exxon pulled out of the county, I don't see a pay increase in our future, so I think I'll apply for a job with the Colorado Springs Police Department. I heard they're accepting applications."

"Yeah…but you don't have to stay in law enforcement. What about the dream or vision you had the first night we slept here? You know, you saw yourself preaching to lots of people?"

"Yeah. I remember. It was pretty weird. But I really think God wants me to be a cop. Besides, if I get hired there, we'll have an instant pay raise. And we'll be close to our families."

"Yeah…but what if we pray for a sign so we'll know for sure it's God's will?"

"Umm…like what?"

"What if we pray that if it's His will, you get the job. If you don't get it, we'll know you're not supposed to work there."

"That sounds good." He led in prayer.

After he applied for the job, we were notified of the testing date. He passed the written test. Then came the physical fitness test. He scored among the top of the group. Next came the psychological test. One more box was checked off the required list. With each test, our parents' and his excitement grew. The CSPD narrowed the remaining qualified people into three different groups. Jamie was in the group to be hired next.

"Looks like we're moving to the Springs!" he announced as he hugged me swinging me around. "There's one more person in the top group. If I don't get the job this time, I'll be first on the list the next time!" We started packing.

A few weeks later, Jamie came home from work despondent. His shoulders sagged. The kids and I met him at the door with hugs and kisses. Sensing his fatigue was worse than usual, I questioned, "What's up, honey?"

After reaching into his back pocket, he withdrew a folded envelope. "This."

"What's that?"

"It's from the Colorado Springs Police Department. They're throwing out the entire test. Everything! There's some lawsuit going on over their hiring process."

Feigning disappointment, I replied, "Oh… I'm sorry, honey. I know how excited you've been."

That's confirmation from God! He wants us in the ministry!

"Nothing I can do about it. Just retest."

My stomach knotted. "You're going to retest? What about our prayer?"

"Our prayer? This has nothing to do with our prayer!" he spat. "It's just a fluke! Yes, I'm going to retest!"

God, I don't understand! We prayed that if it's Your will Jamie would get the job. He didn't. End of story. It's clear as day!

Colorado Springs Police Department notified Jamie about the next testing date. He went through all the same tests month after agonizing month. He finished in the top group this time. He would be hired. We waited day after day for notification of his start date.

Frustrated, Jamie finally called their personnel department. I stopped rinsing the plate in my hand, watching his face as he made the call. "Hi. This is Jamie Royal. I'm waiting to hear about my start date… Uh-hm… Uh-hm… Yes, sir. Okay. I will see you then." A broad smile and thumbs up told me we were moving soon. He hung the phone up. "I got the job! Apparently, their letter was lost in the mail. We have less than two weeks to be packed and moved!"

Scurrying to relocate, we left our condominium up for sale. After eighteen months of testing, he got the job of his dreams. *Lord, it's his dream, but is it Your best for us?*

We rented with the option to buy a lovely house in Green Mountain Falls. The next Sunday we joined the church in Colorado Springs where my in-laws were members. Doubting this was God's will, I didn't agree with the move. Resentment crept into my heart. I was unaware of the infestation.

Lord, I love being close to our parents and going to the new church, but I miss our former church and friends. I can't wipe thoughts of Jamie's dream/vision from my mind.

Determined to fit in, I delved deeply into a ladies' Bible study.

I don't trust Jamie's decisions. Yeah, he got $100 more a month than he was making, but now we've overextended ourselves by renting this house and buying another vehicle.

To make financial ends meet, I found a part-time job. Because Jamie worked nights, I got a day job. We rarely saw one another; our marriage suffered. We hardly had time to give each other a passing peck on the cheek.

Because we left our condominium unsold, debt collectors called several times a day. *Of course, Jamie's in the Colorado Springs Police Academy, so I'm left to deal with the angry callers!* I sobbed after each call.

God allowed a few comical moments; my hubby and I were in our kitchen when he passed a silent but deadly gas "bomb." The scent wafted toward me. Scowling, I shook my head. Just then, two-year-old Shannon entered the room.

Jamie quick-wittedly asked, "Shannon, did you mess your pants?"

We burst into laughter as she pulled down her pants to check.

We prayed and prayed for someone to buy the condominium. After several months, God miraculously sent a buyer. After God showed us to readjust our priorities, we moved from the mountain home to a rental in a suburb of Colorado Springs. Our financial stress reduced; I didn't have to work outside the home. Jamie and I once again enjoyed having time together.

Within one and a half years, we moved into our own home. We placed John in a local Christian kindergarten. Shannon, a very active three-year-old, attended a half-day preschool two mornings a week. Now out of the probationary period, Jamie loved his job. *The 3:00 to 11:00 p.m. shift is pretty much what he worked in Glenwood. I like that back-up and medical care are closer for him.*

God, The Forester, pruned and fertilized me.
As He taught me, my branches grew.

9

John, Shannon, and I regularly walked to the grocery store.

I love kids at this age! They're so gullible!

"Kids, if you scare the doors, they'll open for you!"

They bolted toward the doors screaming, "Argh!"

Poof! Like magic, the doors opened! They strutted, proud of their newfound power.

On evening in early October, a new friend, Maria, came over for dinner. She brought her two-year-old son. Our three kids played, as we laughed and shared easily. A warm fall breeze wafted through the kitchen window. John put on his Superman pajamas. The kids raced back and forth from the kitchen to the living room.

Maria and I stayed in the kitchen while our popcorn finished popping. Suddenly, we heard a crash, and then screams. We bounded toward the wails. John lay behind my room-dividing couch. His leg bent strangely as though no longer attached to his body. I rushed beside him, gently removing his leg from his clothing. His knee was swelling. Just then the phone rang. I asked Maria to answer. She took the call and then handed the phone to me.

I heard my mother-in-law's voice, "Hello? Denise? This is Terri. Who's screaming?"

My voice shakily replied, "It's John. It looks like he twisted his knee. I'm getting ready to drive him to the emergency room."

"This sounds serious! Call an ambulance!"

"Okay."

"Jim and I will head to your house. Why don't you call the ambulance and ask Maria to stay with Shannon 'til we get there?"

"All right. Bye."

I called our ambulance company.

Within minutes, a fire truck, hook and ladder truck, and ambulance arrived. Maria opened the front door. Men rushed into the house and began "stabilizing" my boy. I dialed police dispatch.

"Colorado Springs Police Department. Is this an emergency?"

"Yes. This is Denise Royal. My husband is Officer Jamie Royal on your department. Our son's been hurt. Paramedics are at our house and taking us to Memorial Hospital. Please have Jamie meet me at the hospital."

The paramedics secured a splint under John's leg and began an IV. They believed it wasn't his knee that was hurt, but his thigh, using the term "femur." John continued screaming from pain. I climbed into the ambulance. As the vehicle howled to the hospital, the paramedic said, "Your son might have gone into shock if you'd taken him to the emergency room yourself."

Thank You, God, for the call from Terri!

At the hospital, the staff rapidly wheeled John into an examining room. A doctor rushed to his aid. He quickly grabbed scissors to cut and remove John's underwear.

John screamed, "Not my Superman underwear!" The empathetic doctor tearfully glanced at me.

I held my tears before whispering into John's ear. "I'll buy you more, honey."

X-rays revealed two breaks in John's femur. They formed a triangular shaped break about three inches above his knee. Arriving at the hospital, Jamie entered the room, in full uniform. He stood by my side; his arm held me close.

Doctors began filling the small room. The questioning began, "How did this happen?"

"John stood on the back of our couch, his leg went between the cushion and the frame. He fell behind the couch."

"How tall is your couch?" I raised my hand about three and a half feet off the floor. "About this high," I answered.

"Is your floor carpeted?"

"Yes."

Eyebrows went up among the medical staff. I sensed where their questions were heading.

I'm thankful Maria was at my house when John got hurt. She can be a witness if I'm charged with child abuse.

The next morning, between screams, John mentioned, "The doctors asked me how my leg got broke last night." I nodded. *I figured they would. Detecting possible child abuse is an important part of their job.*

John screamed for two agonizing days, only pausing when pain medicine gave him a few moments of relief. Two days later, surgery was done. A pin was inserted just above his knee for traction. John lie on his back, his broken leg dangling from the traction device for a month.

During the hospital stay, Jamie took his vacation time and we spent as much time as possible with John. Our son had been hospitalized before, but Jamie always had to work. I went through that alone. We were together this time. *It's good to have someone with me. Jamie's presence comforts both John and me.*

John wanted a stuffed animal called a "Pound Puppy" for Christmas; he got that Christmas present early. Once again, family and church members helped babysit, but this time for Shannon.

Our boy was sent home in a body cast for another month. After getting the cast removed, we brought John home from the doctor's office. Immediately, I carried him to the bathroom.

Has it really been two months since he had a bath?

I ran water and sat him in the tub. John instantly fell over. I gasped in horror.

His muscles atrophied so badly; he can't even sit up.

I held him in a sitting position and cried.

John quickly relearned to sit up, crawl, and pull up. Within the first month, he took his first steps; they were unsteady and awkward but...he was walking!

I'm as proud of this triumph as I was of his first tottering toddler steps.

*****

One weekend I drove the kids, ages three and five, up a winding mountain pass. John's comment jolted my attention, "Mom, I think I'm going to do the 'F' word!"

"What? What 'F' word?"

"You know, frow up!"

Smiling, I pulled the car onto the side of the road.

I guess phonics doesn't work very well when you're missing your front teeth!

The next two years passed quickly. One night I had a strange dream. Actually, it wasn't a dream. It was a vision. A voice woke me up. I immediately realized it wasn't a voice from this world, it was very holy.

The voice gently whispered, "God wants to see you in your living room."

Fear paralyzed me. *If I go into God's presence, I'll die! He is Pure Holiness! I'm so filthy!*

The presence repeated, "God wants to see you in your living room."

I can't! I don't want to die! If I just touch Jamie, I'll feel safe. I slowly slid my hand toward my husband. The second I touched him, the vision ended. I lay in bed and cried.

I'm sorry, Lord. I'm sorry I didn't obey! Forgive me. Cleanse me! I'll obey!

The vision didn't return. In spite of the tears, I eventually fell back asleep. The following morning, as I got the kids ready for the day, I questioned, *Lord, what was that about last night?*

God didn't answer. The kids raced through the house. I shrugged. My mind whirled with all the activity around me. I quickly forgot the entire event as life moved forward.

John's mouth was overcrowded as new teeth emerged. Our family dentist warned me of this a year ago when he'd said, "When his next teeth come in, bring him in and I'll pull a tooth to make room for the new one."

I watched for their arrival. *Yep, they're coming in with no room.* The doctor saw us the next week.

On our way for the tooth extraction, I tried to comfort John, "Bet the tooth fairy will give you a whole dollar for this tooth!"

My boy nodded with a grin.

When the doctor quickly pulled the tooth, I exclaimed, "Wow! That's a quick buck!"

The professional's head whipped toward me. "Not you, sir! John's going to get a dollar from the tooth fairy!"

We placed John in the public school's first grade. Jamie's job kept him both busy and challenged. He routinely shared stories from the previous night. He was a natural storyteller, reenacting many events.

Lord, something's different these days about our marriage. There's some kind of enormous chasm between Jamie and me. I can't put my finger on it but everything's different. Jamie and I rarely laugh. The little time we do spend together is strained. He indulges in gifts for himself more and more often. Big, extravagant gifts...a car, a boat. We used to make financial decisions together. Not now. He says, "I deserve this." What can I say? He does deserve them. But how can he buy toys at the expense of our family? I don't understand.

Jamie now had a female partner at work. He spoke of her often. He frequently commented, "She's so funny and kinda cute. You'd really like her. We should have her over one night for supper."

"Hmm, maybe..." Every time I let the conversation drop. *Maybe he'll forget it.*

Within a month, Jamie invited her over for dinner. I tried my best to like her. She was easy to talk to, yet there was something about her that didn't set well with me.

She brings out a different side of Jamie, a side that seems dark, evil, even dirty.

The two of them told inappropriate jokes.

Jamie never talks like this in mixed company. I really don't want to become good friends with this broad. I don't want Jamie spending time with her.

I didn't like Jamie's constant reminders about her and how "incredible" she was. I didn't like that Jamie depended on her for anything, especially his life.

As my jealousy grew, I talked to Jamie, "I don't want you spending any more time with her than what's absolutely necessary."

"I don't understand why that's a problem."

"Well, it just is!" We volleyed the topic back and forth for several minutes. "Promise me you won't spend any off-duty time with her!"

"Okay, I promise that I won't get together with her outside of work."

"Good."

One day after going to the gym with her dad, Shannon innocently quipped, "I saw Daddy's friend today."

"You did? What's his name?" I inquired.

"No, silly! It's not a boy. It's a girl!" she laughed at my ignorance.

"A girl? What's her name?"

"You know, she ate dinner with us one night."

Unbelievable, it's his work partner. The one he agreed not to see outside of work. Anger welled up inside me. As soon as we had time alone, I confronted Jamie. "Shannon told me she met your friend at the gym."

His gaze went to the floor. "Yeah, about that..."

"The one you told me, no, you promised me that you wouldn't see outside of work!"

"Yeah, I'm sorry. It won't happen again."

How can I trust you now?

At church, I was the perfect wife and mother. I excelled in every class. The kids and I went to everything our church offered:

Sunday School, Sunday morning worship service, Tuesday night visitation, and Wednesday night prayer service. I was even enrolled in a challenging course called "Continuing Witness Training." This class required a copious amount of memorization. I led people to the Lord. I wanted to be the best Christian I could be. I'd joined every committee I could.

Occasionally, Jamie and I filled in as teachers for our class of young married couples. When asked, we even counseled them. Yet I refused to allow people to see the discontentment that'd woven its way around my heart.

I hate that Jamie took this stupid job! Other husbands are home every night, home every holiday, and coach T-ball. They're also home on weekends and can be at church every week. What about the "vision" Jamie had that first night in our condominium before Shannon was born? What if God wanted us in the ministry? Jamie would make an excellent pastor. I would make a great preacher's wife. Our marriage would be perfect if only...

In spite of my agitation with Jamie's job, I believed I was growing closer to God. Instead, my pride grew.

When people see my family, they probably think we have our lives together.

I refused to see that I relied on myself to make things appear wonderful—much like I used to do in high school, before I accepted Jesus as my Lord and Savior.

The ultimate Arborist was still good.
My roots dove deeper into the earth as He nurtured me.

*****

Yet, as a tree I had boastful thoughts.
"Look how tall I am! See how full my branches are!
So many birds and animals depend on me!"

10

After my trip down memory lane, my mind returns to present reality. I thank God for my experiences at the women's conference and remember the commitment card tucked safely in my bottom vanity drawer.

Thoughts fill my mind. *I can't wait till this fall when both kids will be in school! Jamie and I will be alone together for the first time since John was born!*

I ponder the last two years. Something's changed in our marriage. *Maybe things will be better this year. Maybe Jamie and I will get along better.* I nestle into my recliner. *It's good to be home.*

I can't imagine the enemy's twisted plans, nor how God will use this simple retreat commitment card to show His care and provision.

*****

A few months later, we go on a camping vacation at a local lake. We fish and swim. The kids and Jamie water ski.

We haven't had this much fun in years! Maybe this vacation is just what we need to revive our marriage!

Yet thoughts still linger, nagging at my heart.

Our marriage is still struggling. Jamie's changed. He no longer cares about attending church or spending daily time with his Lord.

One night at church, alone again, at the service's ending, God deeply convicts me to pray for our marriage. I go to the altar and kneel. Crying, I pray. *Lord, I give you my marriage. I ask You to bring*

Jamie to Yourself no matter what the cost. I totally surrender to Your will. I'm tired of the gap between Jamie and me, tired of having little in common spiritually. Have Your way in my life, and our marriage.

Several weeks pass. We celebrate our ninth anniversary. We go to a movie and out for dinner. *He doesn't really want to be here. He doesn't like to even spend time with me! He's doing this out of obligation not love.*

We hardly exchanged two sentences over dinner.

Nine years. Hooray for us. Lord, help us be what You want us to be.

A good friend, Leslie, stops by a week later. For the first time, I'm able to share about my concerns for my marriage. I tell of the on-going emotional separation between us.

"I'm afraid Jamie had an affair two years ago. Maybe it was with a coworker."

"Do you have any evidence?"

"No."

"Do you have anything concrete to go on?"

"No."

"Why don't we pray about this for a week? Then, if you still feel this way, confront Jamie."

"All right. Thanks. It's probably nothing." She leads us in prayer then leaves.

That evening I become obsessively jealous. I can't get my mind to think about anything else.

If Jamie had an affair two years ago, I'll forgive him and we'll move on.

I pray. *God, please help me speak with Jamie. If it's Your will for me to talk with him tonight, then have me be awake when he comes home from work.*

After putting the kids to bed, I read my Bible and watch TV. Later, as I crawl into bed, the phone rings. It's a neighbor. She's crying. "Denise, would you pray with me about my marriage problems?"

How ironic!

We talk for over an hour. As I hang up the phone, I hear the garage door open. Within seconds, I hear Jamie enter the kitchen. I hesitate, say a quick, silent prayer, and get out of bed. Slinging my robe around my shoulders, I head to the kitchen. Jamie's head is in the fridge, as he checks for leftovers.

"Jamie, I need to talk with you."

"Okay, let me get a snack and I'll be right to bed."

"No, Jamie, I need to talk now. Come, sit down."

He glances up. "Okay." Seeing I was serious, he sits across from me at our kitchen table. "What's up?"

I take a deep breath. "Jamie, I need to know if you've ever had an affair."

Shock registers in his eyes, and his expression changes. His glance becomes glued to the table. He whispers, "Yes."

"When?" I ask.

I know when—two years ago.

"Last week."

Somehow, I remain in control.

Last week?

My mind tries to understand what he said.

Last week...

Calmness engulfs me.

"Ask him if there was any other time," a familiar Voice gently prods.

"Any other time?" I mechanically probe.

"Yes."

Yes? I feel like someone just punched my gut.

"When?" I counter.

"Two years ago."

"Was it with your coworker?"

"No."

My voice begins to quake. "Then who?"

He tells me of the girl he knew for a long time. "It was Susan. She looked me up and called me."

"Susan? The gal you dated before we met? You're still in contact with her?" I inhaled slowly. *Oh boy. I wasn't ready for that.*

At this revelation Jamie's eyes tear up. He stands; punches the wall over our stove. A picture falls off the wall. Its glass shatters. "I'm so sorry! I won't ever do it again. I'll do whatever it takes to make you believe me!"

"Leave. Pack your clothes and get out!"

He hangs his head in defeat, turns and does exactly what I demand, packs his clothes, and leaves.

As soon as he walks out, I start shaking and crying. I decide to shower.

I feel disgustingly dirty. I've got to be clean of the filth that's come into our lives.

I stand in the corner of the shower, water running, and continue weeping. I end up in a heap on the shower floor.

After dragging myself out of the shower, I dry, dress, and pick up the phone. I call Leslie. I recognize her husband's groggy voice when he answers the phone. "Hello?" I have no idea what time it is. I don't even care.

"I…*sniff*…need…to…*sniff*…talk…to…uh…Leslie." I stammer between sobs.

"Hello?" Leslie questions.

"It's all true!" I exhale into the phone.

"Denise? Is this you?"

I manage to eke out, "Yeah." Then I melt into another bout of uncontrollable blubbering.

"I'll be right over."

Leslie is at my house within fifteen minutes. She holds me as I collapse into her embrace. I'm not sure how long she stays with me. "I've got to get home now. I have to be at my house to get the kiddos breakfast when they wake up. I'll call you in a little bit."

"Okay." After closing the door, I make my way to my bed.

"I stay in bed until the alarm rings. I climb out of bed to get my kids ready for Vacation Bible School. This was the first year since I was a teenager that I'd not volunteered to help. I felt that God told me not to teach or help at all this year. I hadn't known why. I drive the kids to our church and drop them off.

As I open our house's front door, an incredible, hollow loneliness sweeps over me. I pick up the phone and call our pastor. "I need you to come over. Jamie had an affair." I state before beginning to cry softly.

He arrives shortly. After entering our house, he jerks the front curtains open. My heart cringes.

Don't do that! Everyone will see! Everyone will know!

I pull my emotions together momentarily.

"What's going on, Denise? How can I help?"

"Jamie had an affair! Please pray for us!"

He bows his head and prays. He and his wife take John, Shannon, and me out for lunch when I pick the kids up from Vacation Bible School.

That evening Jamie calls and tells me about a marriage counselor our pastor recommended.

At least he cares enough to call the pastor.

I agree to go see him the next day.

Lord, I've never faced this before. I need someone to give us direction.

That evening I crawl into bed for another long sleepless night.

The following day, I take the kids to Bible school and return to the house.

I hate it here! I hate the silence! I hate the smell! I hate everything I once called "home!"

Slowly, I walk through the living room and into the kitchen. Something crunches under my feet. It's a piece of glass from the picture Jamie broke the first night. As I kneel to pick it up, I crumple into a heap on the floor.

My world's disintegrating! I perform the actions of being a mom with no emotions. I function only as a robot. My mind refuses to work beyond the simplest tasks. Jamie comes home later that day and drives us to the professional's office.

Once inside, the man hands us some papers. "Fill these out, and then we'll talk."

"Okay," Jamie answers. I can't even look up from the floor.

The pages contain personality tests. The expert reappears. "You finished?"

Jamie glances at me before answering, "Yes, sir."

"Come on in my office. We'll go over the results. Denise, it says here that your husband helps around the house?"

"That's right," I reply.

"It also states that he helps with the kids."

"Yes."

"So what are you here for? Does nothing make you happy?"

Is he serious?

I flatly answer, "We're here because my husband had an affair."

"Yes, but…" the counselor begins a lecture. I completely block the words out. I can see his lips moving but it's as though I'm deaf. When I finally re-engage my mind, he's still talking. *Concentrate! We came seeking direction; I need to listen.*

"So… I want you to go home and think of everyone you know who really has a need. Think of what you can do to help them. You've got to get your mind off of yourself." *Have I just stepped into a strange movie? This can't be my life, my marriage he's blabbering about.*

He continues droning on and on, "You should let Jamie move back in immediately! Nothing should change in your marriage! I repeat, nothing! Resume normal intimacy. You should tell no one. You shouldn't have called your pastor!"

He states one nugget of gold to which I cling: "Either you can teach Jamie a lesson or let God teach him. If you teach him it won't last, if God teaches him, it'll last forever."

Is God still good? I don't deserve this! I did everything right so we'd have a good marriage! I kept my vows. I obeyed God. Does he see? Does he hear? Does he care? Where is He?

The Forester surveys His strong, tall, straight tree.
"This is perfect now. The time has come. You have My permission."
Quickly, I glance down as a sharp blow strikes my body's trunk.
The Forester's allowing me to be cut down!
Help! Somebody, help! Why's this happening?
I don't understand! How can this be within my Creator's plan?
The forest trembles as I forcefully hit the cold, unforgiving sod.

11

Jamie moves back in immediately. Life resumes as though nothing has happened: nothing except my life ended. This man jerked my dreams out of my arms and butchered them. I sleep and even have a "normal" sex life with the murderer. I know I'll never go back to that counselor. The only thing I feel he said that was worthwhile was, "If you teach Jamie, it won't last. If God teaches him, it will last forever." Although unsure of his advice to "not tell anyone," I keep my mouth shut. I desperately plead. *God teach him. I want this lesson to last.*

My close friend continues reaching out to me. She and her family invite the kids and me over regularly for dinner. She comes over every day that first month. She makes sure I get out of bed. She drives me to get groceries, go to the bank, everyday routine things. My grief's so deep and black my mind can barely function. Leslie and her family help by simply being there and being willing to listen. Above all, they give me shoulders on which to cry.

Music's a thing of the past in our home. I refuse to sing or play any music on the stereo. Why sing? There's nothing but pain, sorrow, and betrayal!

Our children know nothing about what is going on between us. One night as I retreat to get a warm bath, I overhear our daughter ask, "Daddy, why's Mommy crying?"

Jamie softly replies, "Well, I hurt Mommy real bad. She'll be okay, but right now she just needs some time alone."

Jamie starts both reading his Bible and praying. Although I'm glad to see him dive into God's Word, I won't open my own. *Lord, I feel deserted by You! I know You could've kept this from happening to me! I'm obedient to You! You didn't protect me at all!*

Jamie asks, "Would you start reading the Bible with me?"

"No!" The thought turns my stomach.

Jamie faithfully reads his Bible daily. He takes the kids to church without me. He grows stronger spiritually, gradually becoming the spiritual leader of our home again.

About every other week, Jamie's discouragement erupts, "I may as well leave!"

"Please stay. Things will get better." *Why do I have to comfort him? Why won't he just hold and console me?*

*****

I write in my journal, "Lord, please be with me. I feel as though I'm drowning, as though Satan's storms are attacking from every side, beating me with fierce winds. Lord, I feel weak and vulnerable. Please shelter me as You did the psalmist. Place Your hedge around me. Don't let Satan defeat me. I love You, Lord!"

Mom and Dad call weekly. Although they're very busy with the church Dad pastors, I know they'd be by my side if I tell them. I don't. Instead, I lie. I'm usually crying when they call. "Denise, you sound like you've got a cold. Are you okay?"

"Yeah," I sniffle. "My sinuses are just all messed up."

"Okay. Let us know if you need anything."

One afternoon John and Shannon are riding their bikes in front of our house. I'm starting to cook dinner when suddenly the front door's thrown open. John darts into the kitchen, "Mom! Shannon's hurt! She's lying in the street! Come quick!"

I race out the front door to Shannon lying in the street. She's conscious. Blood's flowing from her head. As I kneel beside her, I ask, "Are you okay, Shannon?" She doesn't answer. Her eyes are glazed, her expression, confused. I carefully lift her off the street; I gently place her on our grass. "John, stay here while I get my keys." When I return, Shannon is sitting up.

She asks, "What happened?"

Explaining, I place her on the back seat. "You fell off your bike. We're taking you to the hospital. John, I need you to sit by Shannon."

Shannon repeatedly asks, "What happened?" as I speed to the hospital.

The ER doctor checks on Shannon. "I'm ordering a CAT scan. I'll be back when we get the results." Several hours later he returns. "Everything looks okay medically but she's suffered a concussion. We want to keep her overnight for observation."

As soon as the doctor's words were out of his mouth, Shannon sits up and screams, "I'm going to die! I'm going to die if I stay here! I'm gonna die!" John pales.

Attempting to calm her, I hug her. "No, honey. You're not going to die. Everything will be all right. You'll be okay."

After arriving in her appointed room, Shannon's eyes survey the environment. The nurse quickly brings a popsicle and hands it to Shannon, stating, "This is your dinner." A mischievous smile immediately appears on her five-year-old angelic face. With bright, smiling eyes she excitedly ponders, "Wonder what's for breakfast!"

Within days of Shannon being discharged from the hospital, the kids and I begin getting ready for school. We shop for the needed clothes and school supplies.

One morning Jamie states, "I think we need to change churches. Why don't we try the one down the street?" Still emotionally numb, I wordlessly shrug.

I feel like garbage being pushed around by a broom. Why does it matter?

We join a closer church. The pastor and his wife seem sweet. We meet new people. One day, a young lady comes by our house. I share with her about our marriage problems. She graciously prays with me and agrees to pray regularly for me.

Several weeks after God showed me about the affair, one evening as Jamie and I talk, I noticed that his wedding ring's broken.

Shocked, I scream, "Get that ring off your finger! I don't want to see you wear it until you get it fixed!"

The ring symbolizes our marriage. The cracked gold is an ugly reminder of our dying relationship.

Great, even his ring shows impending doom.

"I'll get it fixed tomorrow!" Jamie tries to comfort. Keeping his word, he makes a trip to a jeweler the next day. The ring's repaired while he waits.

A few more days pass. I find more broken glass from that first night. Wanting to stay numb, I try my best to stuff all of my emotions out of sight.

One afternoon, I walk out to our mailbox and grab our new letters, bills, and ads. After walking back into the house, I sit at our dining room table. I normally go through the bills, checking to make sure they're all correct. As I look through our phone bill, an unusual number catches my eye. *Hmm, I don't recognize that one.* I casually throw it aside.

I'll ask Jamie about it later. He might know who that was.

When he gets home from work that night, I ask, "Do you recognize this number?"

His head and gaze go down immediately. My stomach knots with sudden realization.

"Yeah," he whispered, "that's her number."

I shout, "You called her from here?!"

He nods, keeping his eyes fixed on the floor.

"Where was I?"

He mumbles, "You were taking a bath."

"Where were the kids?"

"They were in bed."

"That's it!" I yell, slinging the dish towel I'm holding to the floor. "I want to know everything. No more secrets. I need to know everything that happened...where you went, what you did, everything." I jerk out a chair. Glaring, I plop down.

"You don't really want to know."

"Oh, yeah… I do. But first, I want you to call her. Tell her it's over between the two of you. You never want to hear from her again.""

"But she's a nice girl! I don't want to hurt her feelings."

My cheeks burn from anger. "You're concerned about her feelings?" Not mine?

"No, I'll call her." I hand Jamie the phone. "Right now?"

"Yes, and I will be on the other phone-line listening."

Jamie makes the call. He and she speak awkwardly, but he states the words I'd demanded.

"Okay, now tell me everything."

He patiently tells me everything, answers every question, and takes every insult. Sadness engulfs me. The weight's an anchor pulling me deeper and deeper into a chasm. Immediately, my brain categorizes this person as an enemy. The "enemy" is real. She's been in my house! She's seen my children's pictures! She slept with my husband in our bed! Chills encompass me.

The trembling continues day and night. I often wake screaming from nightmares. I don't remember what I dreamed. Life's intolerable as the enemy relentlessly torments me.

Summer finally changes to fall. School is about to start. I had looked forward to this time of Jamie and me having time alone together for so long. Now I enter this period with a dulled heart, absent of emotions.

God speaks to me clearly one day. "Denise, if you keep depending on Me, I will make sure this won't be as painful. If you refuse My guidance, things will be horrible."

I bristle against Him, emphatically tell Him, "No! I am through trusting You! You didn't protect me at all! I obeyed You! I did everything right! Absolutely not! I will not trust you!"

Immediately, pain sears through my heart. The organ feels ripped into two pieces. I grasp my chest as agony courses through every inch of flesh. The relentless sensation takes both my energy and breath away.

Within a few days I decide. *I've had enough! There's no reason to prolong the inevitable! I'm done! I'll be dead within the week.*

Two days before Jamie's next day off work, I stop eating and drinking. I daily grow weaker. I begin having scary hallucinations. By the third morning, I can't even get out of bed. I hear the phone ring.

I don't care who it is. I am not talking to anyone!

Jamie taps gently on our bedroom door. "Denise, it's Leslie. She wants to talk to you."

"Tell her I'm not up to talking."

"Okay." I hear Jamie's muffled voice as he walks down the hall. Within five minutes the phone rings again. Jamie speaks, "Denise, it's Leslie again. She says she's going to keep calling until she hears your voice."

"Fine. Give me the phone. 'Hi, Leslie.'"

"Are you okay?"

"Fine. Don't call again."

"You don't sound fi—"

I hang up.

Shock causes Jamie to raise his voice. "You just hung up on your best friend!"

I spit, "Get out of here! Just leave me alone!" Covering my head, I curl into a tighter ball.

Jamie gently closes the door. Within fifteen minutes the same door's thrown open so hard it hits the wall behind it. I hear Leslie's angry voice. "How dare you hang up on me!" She jerks the covers off my head. "When was the last time you ate?" I shrug. "Have you even been drinking anything?" Another shrug is my only response. "I'll be right back!"

I hear her stomp down the hall and back again. "Sit up!" Physically, I can't. Leslie's tone softens, "Oh, Denise!" She helps me sit up. "Here, I brought you some water. Drink a few sips. Oh, Denise! I'll help you hold the glass! Just a few sips at a time, there you go. Good, good. Let that settle in your stomach. Good. Now let's get you out of this bed." She gently grasps my arm, helping me stand. "There. Get your balance. That's good. I'll help you into your bathroom. There you go. I'll give you a few minutes of privacy…now let's go into your kitchen and I'll get you something to eat."

Shaking my head, I hesitate.

"This isn't an option. I am going to make you some food and you are going to eat." Her hand tightens slightly on my arm as she leads me to the kitchen.

Leslie patiently sits across the table watching me eat every bite. She stays for almost an hour. *She's probably making sure I don't throw it up.* The love and concern she exudes make my eyes fill with tears. I meekly whisper, "Thank you."

"I'll bring you dinner tonight. Then when you're stronger, you and your kids will eat dinner with me and my kids for a few nights."

"Thank you."

Leslie keeps her promise. She sits with John, Shannon, and me as we eat.

"I'll be by tomorrow around five to pick you up. See you later!" She shuts the door as she leaves.

At dinner, Leslie states, "You and the kids can come again tomorrow night for supper."

"Are you sure?"

"Absolutely."

"Okay. I think I can drive tomorrow."

"All right. It's a date."

The kids and I eat at their house regularly. Les comes over every day for the next month.

One afternoon, the doorbell rings. A new friend from church is standing outside holding a wrapped gift.

"Hi, can you come in?"

"I can't stay, but just want to drop off something. God told me to buy this for you."

"Okay. Can I open it now?"

"If you want!"

I gingerly open the package. Inside is a cassette tape. I weakly smile and humbly state, "Thank you."

"Hope you enjoy it. Praying for you! Bye!" she yells as she runs to her mini-van.

As I rest that afternoon, I decide to listen to the tape. The music is by the singer, Evie. I know about her but don't own any of her music. Two of the songs speak to me, "Special Delivery" and "Never Alone Again."

Listening to those songs daily, I cling to the Lord's promises they hold. I won't pray anymore. Yet somehow these songs become my silent pleas. I secretly hope God hears them.

One morning I'm pecking a few songs on my piano, when Jamie sits down beside me. He begins singing the hymn I'm playing. *Lord, how many years have I waited for him to join me?* My heart reluctantly thanks God for the small miracle.

*****

A couple weeks later, I walk John and Shannon to school. John's now in second grade, Shannon, kindergarten. The weather's beautiful.

Inwardly, I grieve.

This was supposed to be our time. Everything should be perfect. Instead, he ruined it!

As we wait for the first bell to ring, I notice a mother and child approaching.

I've seen them at our new church.

I guide my kids toward them. "Hi. I'm Denise Royal. Did you and your husband recently join the church on the corner?"

"Yes! I'm Angel and this is Meaghan, my daughter. We just moved to Colorado." After exchanging phone numbers, we take our girls into their class.

Now that the kids are in school, I have more time to contemplate my mess. Jamie and I have more time together. I hate it. We fight, or I should say, I vehemently accuse Jamie daily. I spit putrid vile insults. They erupt from my heart and spew through my lips. I hate myself. I hate Jamie. I will not, cannot sit at the same table with him. *I don't want to talk to him, let alone look at him.*

On the few weekends Jamie has a day off, I make myself sit with the kids and their dad during meals.

One day, I tell Jamie I have to get away. Hoping to shake him up and let him know how serious his offense is, I grab my gun from its normal spot, and the car keys off the table. Then I drive out of the city. As I leave town, I look for a place to end it all—the pain, the hatefulness, the heartache. As I drive, I sense I'm not alone. It seems there's a war going on around me, as though beings not quite human are fighting for my life. With no resolution, I eventually turn around to go back home.

Later that week I shop for groceries. Sticking to my normal routine, I drive to every store having a sale on the items on my grocery list. After completing that mission, I hurriedly unload the car. I glance at my watch. *Yikes! Time to go get the kids!* I race to the car and drive to pick the kids up from school.

That night, as I put on my nightgown, the fabric catches on my engagement ring.

That's strange!

My mouth drops open as I glance down to see open prongs where my engagement diamond should be. I carefully shake my gown and then clothes. Nothing happens.

I run to the kitchen plundering through the groceries. I begin rummaging through the drawers, trash, and refrigerator. I race to the garage. I dig through the car. Still there was no sign of my diamond.

My stone's gone; no doubt about it.

Defeat cast a leaden weight on me as I trudge back into the house. My shoulders heave, lungs emit loud sobs, as I sink to the floor.

How much more am I going to have to lose?

The pain is as fresh as when I first heard Jamie say he'd had an affair.

One more part of my marriage is gone. Is everything I ever held dear going to be stripped away?

One day Leslie drives me to my bank. I dry my eyes before entering. Stepping into the establishment, I notice a uniformed police officer standing in the teller's line. My spine stiffens. I freeze. "Denise, you okay?" Leslie questions.

A cop. Great. They're all just a bunch of cheaters!

"Uh, yeah." Hearing her voice brings my mind back to reality. After completing my transaction, we return to her vehicle.

Once inside Leslie speaks again, "It was the police officer, wasn't it?"

I turn my head slowly toward her, nodding. Tears fill my eyes. "Yeah." I whisper.

"I'm so sorry."

Several months later, I realize I rely too heavily on Leslie and Dave. I pile my sorrow on their shoulders. One evening Dave states, "Denise, you need to leave Jamie."

"I can't."

"We love you. We hate seeing you in constant pain. Leave him. You deserve better."

"I won't."

Our friendship never recovers. I don't know why I don't tell them, "God told me to stay."

Invitations to their house and for help come less frequently. I understand. They love me too much to watch the debilitating pain.

Before I can eat at the same table with Jamie, his birthday arrives. *Great.* His family comes to help us "celebrate." The long day's awkward and miserable.

I can't stand to eat in the same room with him. How am I supposed to be happy about the day he was born? Somehow, I muddle through the day.

Weeks later, it's my birthday. I write in my journal, "Happy Birthday. I'm twenty-eight years old today and have hit rock bottom. I guess and hope the only way left to go is up. I can't pray or seem to get close to God. What scares me even more is I'm not sure if I want to. I'm still afraid to get close to Jamie—to trust him—I'm afraid it'll all be for nothing. Again, Lord, if You can and will…help."

A few days later, I receive a phone call from the new girl from school and church. She wants to get together. "Yes, we can come over after school." So begins our friendship. She's a Christian needing a friend. I'm a…mess and need… I don't know what… I suppose it's a miracle.

Suddenly a strong hand places me on a firm surface.
My last memory was standing tall in the woods.
"Behold!" a Voice booms.
"What will I see?" I pry my eyes open.
The radiant light hurts my eyes.
Slowly, my gaze rises to view my reflection in a large mirror.
Horrified, I shriek,
"I'm a violin? Why a violin?
I can't believe it!
I don't even like violins!
They're the whiniest instrument I've ever heard!"

12

Although life's daily routines resume, I struggle with everything. I have no energy, motivation, or joy.

What am I supposed to do? I can't bring myself to do his laundry, let alone pray for him.

A few weeks later, Jamie comes home from work early. He's on crutches.

"What happened to you?"

Jamie eases himself into his recliner. "I was chasing a felon, and stepped in a hole. We got the guy, but my ankle's broken. I'm off for a couple of weeks."

Great, now I have to wait on him.

Two long weeks later, Jamie's back at work, assigned to "light duty." One afternoon, as he leaves for work, I feel uneasy.

Something's going to happen today. I don't know what, but something's going to happen to Jamie at work.

I wish I could kneel and pray for him, but I don't. My heart's cold and bitter toward the man who betrayed me.

Late that afternoon the kids are outside playing when the phone rings. "Hello."

A solemn male voice asks, "Mrs. Royal?"

"Yes…"

"This is Memorial Hospital. Your husband is here. We need you to come and bring him clothes and shoes."

"Okay. Can I speak to him?"

"No. He can't get to the phone."

I cringe. *Things have to be bad for him not to be able to talk on the phone.*

I robotically reply, "Okay, I'll be right there."

Who can watch the kids? I call Angel. "Can you watch my kids? Jamie's been hurt."

"Sure, bring them over."

I speed to the hospital. Entering the parking garage, I slow our car to a crawl. The Emergency Room entrance is blocked by a barrage of police vehicles.

This can't be good.

Shakily, I enter. The emergency room lobby and hall are packed with police officers.

This doesn't look good. Swallowing, I take a deep breath.

Squeezing into a large exam room, I push through a battalion of uniformed men. I make my way to where Jamie lays. His hair's no longer blond, but is now matted reddish-brown, clinging to his scalp.

The jacket and vest of the three-piece suit he wore to work this morning are missing.

The bottom part of his cast is also gone, as is the shoe from his good foot. He's stripped down to his t-shirt which this morning was bleached white, but is now the same color as his hair.

I recognize the familiar sight: dried blood.

Trying not to faint, I lean against the cold wall, slowly inhaling. I continue pushing through the uniformed bodies toward Jamie.

After making my way to his side, I lean forward. "Is this your blood or the other guy's?"

"The other guy's."

Relieved, I backed through the uniforms. Leaning against a wall, I draw a deep breath.

Several hours later, the doctor informs us that Jamie's cleared to be released from the hospital. A coworker volunteers to drive him to the office where several officers will interview him about the altercation. I drive myself home.

Hours later, Jamie enters our front door. Immediately I confront him as his shaky, exhausted form enters. I coldly state, "Well, I figured out one thing from all of this."

"Oh, yeah? What's that?"

"I figured out that I don't want you dead." I turn without another word, leaving the injured man leaning on his crutches at the front door, and go to bed.

*****

The next Sunday, we get ready to go to our new church. Since we're still new to these church members, people try not to stare at Jamie.

I always enjoy seeing people's reactions to awkward situations. Gazes scrutinize Jamie's broken nose, scrapes down his neck, scabbed knuckles, black eyes, and casted leg. Then they regard me, his small, quiet wife. No one asks a question. No one says a word. They don't know Jamie's profession. He looks like he's been in a bad bar fight.

As we drive home, I bring up the subject, "Did you see how everyone stared at us?"

"Yeah! But no one asked me what happened!"

"Wonder what they were thinking! Maybe they thought I beat you up!"

Laughter breaks out between us and overflows to our kids. It's good to laugh together.

Yet I still can't bring myself to meet people's eyes. Shame overwhelms me.

My husband chose to abandon our vows. He chose someone else. I'm not enough for him. I failed at one of his basic, core needs. I'm not worthy of my marriage. Shame invisibly drapes over me. Its weight's as heavy as a doused blanket.

If other people look into my eyes, they'll see my pain, my failure. Will they also be able to see into my soul?

A few days later, I spot another piece of broken glass.

You've got to be kidding! How long will this go on?

Every shard found is another miserable reminder of my broken marriage.

There's no purpose to live. My marriage is over. I stretched my friendship with Leslie too far. That's gone now too.

Once again, I resolve to stop my pain. I tell Jamie I won't be home, grab my Bible, gun, car keys and leave. I drive to a local motel determined to either hear from God or end my life. Upon entering the hotel room, I break down and sob. After melting to the floor beside the bed, I pull my Bible toward me and pray. *Lord, I need to hear from You. Please give me a word. Show me something!* I thumb through my Bible until I get to 1 Peter.

I read until I feel God's tender embrace. The words of one verse seem to stand apart from all the others. I read 1 Peter 5:10 (NIV): "And the God of all grace, who called you to his eternal glory in Christ, after you have suffered a little while, will Himself restore you and make you strong, firm, and steadfast." I reread the verse.

God Himself will restore you after you've suffered a little while. *How long is a "little while?"*

I wipe my tears and pack my things. *Okay, Lord. Once again, let's do this together.* His peace envelops me. My soul feels new strength. My trembling slows, although my heart still aches.

Two weeks before my sister and her family are due to come home for Thanksgiving, Shannon breaks out with chickenpox.

Of course, what else? I should've expected it. This is the cherry on top of the toxic sundae.

Three days before my daughter clears up, John breaks out. Our company arrives the next day. Cindy, Jeff, and their kids stay with us for part of their visit. We try to keep the cousins apart. We believe we've done a good job. Two weeks later, her daughter comes down with chickenpox. Gradually, like dominoes, the virus spreads, taking its turn through all three of her kids.

I do my best to follow the counselor's advice. I don't tell anyone what's going on in my home or heart. It's a very difficult holiday. As sisters, we're usually close. Not telling Cindy what's going on is almost impossible. Still in an emotional blur, they leave before I hardly know they were here.

The following month passes slowly as Christmas approaches.

How can I put the tree up? How can I shop for gifts?

I decide I won't decorate. I'm not sure it was really a conscious decision. I just can't bring myself to do it.

One afternoon, Jamie asks, "Honey? When do you plan to decorate the tree?"

"I don't!"

Later that day, I'm shocked to see Jamie unpacking our tree. This is the first time in our marriage he's done anything to get ready for Christmas. Now, he silently decorates the tree.

Christmas morning comes and goes, almost as unobserved and unremembered as my sister's visit. I'm glad to have the kids for a diversion. Jamie and I sit on opposite sides of the kids as they unwrap their presents. Christmas music plays softly on the stereo. Hardly a word's spoken between Jamie and me. Everything centers on the kids. We go to his parents for a very strained meal. They know about our problems. I sense they're hurting as well. Yet nothing's stated. Everything remains hushed and ignored.

I don't remember how long the Christmas decorations were up or who took them down. The old year's tragedy forever sears my memory.

How will I ever face the new one?

I can't comprehend the thought.

Last year was horrible, absolutely horrible. My strength's totally gone.

Painfully, the year ends.

Maybe the New Year will be better. Maybe, but I doubt it.

A small hand gingerly grasps my violin neck.
I seem too heavy for this person.
Slowly the musician begins practicing regularly.
A whining dirge reverberates through my empty hull.
Shoulders tighten from the squeaking.
Yes, just as I expected—screechy and whiny.

13

A few days after school resumes, my phone rings. It's the new girl. "Hi, Denise, it's Angel. Would you and your kids like to come over after school for some cookies?"

"Sure, that sounds fun."

After she and I pick our students up from school, we walk to her rental. She and I talk easily. I like her. She a real person, she doesn't put up false fronts. She shares with me about difficulties she's having. God opens my mouth and I'm able to really share private things about my marriage. She cries with me, prays with me.

Her name is Angel. Amazing! Did God send her my direction for such a time as this?

After months of leaning heavily on Leslie's friendship, our relationship hit a major obstacle. These dear friends repeatedly tell me to leave Jamie. It's impossible for me to continue exposing them to my raw pain without following their advice. I know their intention is good. They just can't bear the pain they see each day. God isn't giving them the direction He gives me.

Leslie has such a tender heart. Yet I know God wants me to stay in my marriage for now.

Sadly, I break off our friendship.

A few days later, I decide to play my piano. Dad bought and restored it when I was a junior in high school. My parents gave it to me when Jamie and I bought our first place. Although it's a beautiful piece of furniture, it can't hold a tune. Several keys make no sound whatsoever. I pull an old hymnal from the piano bench and begin playing.

"Ugh! This piano is disgusting! I'm sick of not having anything nice!" I complain as Jamie enters the living room. "I want another piano."

"Huh?" Jamie jerks his coffee cup from his lips. "Well…they're pretty expensive."

"Yeah. They are. It doesn't have to be new. We can get a used one. I also want to take some more piano lessons."

"Hm, that'll cost quite a bit."

"Not quite as much as a car or boat."

"You're right. Start looking in the paper."

Within a few weeks I find a Spinet for sale. Jamie drives me to the residence. I sit on the bench and play one of the only songs I know.

It sounds heavenly!

"Jamie, what do you think?"

"If you want it, it's yours," he shrugs as he smiles.

I jump up and give him a high-five.

It's delivered within a few days.

I sell my upright. Although owning it brought precious memories of my dad, my heart says it's time to move forward.

Sylvia, a music director from a previous church, agrees to instruct me at my house weekly.

I doubt she knows what refuge I find sitting under her tutelage.

Slowly, I let music back into our house, my life. Practicing took my mind off my anger. My playing marginally improves.

One evening, I earnestly pray, *God, I'll stay in my marriage if You'll promise that this will never happen again.*

I hear His voice immediately, not audibly, but clearly in my heart nonetheless. "I won't promise that it won't happen again. Jamie still has free will. I do promise that I'll be with you no matter what happens. I'll take care of you."

Tears well up and overflow. I humbly bow my head in complete surrender. *Okay, Lord. I'll stay as long as You want me to stay.*

Ever so slowly I eat at the same table with Jamie. Gradually we're able to laugh together. The days and months move sluggishly along. Somehow, we're still together. I begin seeing some good in Jamie, little by little.

My new friend, Angel, soon moves across the street. We get together daily, sharing, crying, and sometimes laughing. Our friendship brings healing into my life. Our husbands work opposite shifts, but hers always welcomes me and the kids. We regularly eat dinner at their home. Our girls become best friends.

Time passes. Little by little God heals most of my pain. God renews love, joy, and music in our home. One evening, as I'm taking a bath, God speaks to my heart and gives me a song—both words and tune.

"Nothing Grows on the Mountain Top"

Once I questioned the trials this life brings.
My eyes beheld the mountainous scenes.
In the valley is pain and suffering.
Lord, I wish that you would intervene.
The mountain top is peaceful and free…
Place my heart there so I can see Thee.
As I sulked o'er my sorry fate—
This is what I heard my Lord state.
Nothing grows on the mountaintop,
Nothing grows on the mountaintop.
In the valley far below,
Is where all things thrive and grow.
Then I looked at the mountain top once more.
And my soul began to soar.
It was true what He said to me…
On the mountain top there were no trees.
Then I knew that the valley was the place
To teach me His love, patience, and grace.
Looking back at the hard times that I've known,

I can see that's when I've really grown.
For,
Nothing grows on the mountain top,
Nothing grows on the mountain top.
In the valley far below,
Is where all things thrive and grow.

*****

As the months pass, Jamie becomes accustomed to taking me to the emergency room. My heart constantly physically aches. I often experience rapid heartbeats that leave me exhausted and weak. *Am I having a heart attack? None of the multitude of doctors I see find anything wrong.* Test after test are performed. Nothing abnormal shows up. Weakness pervades every muscle of my body. *I've dealt with this ever since I refused God's comfort. I vividly remember that first stabbing, flesh tearing throb.* Now it never leaves, just varies in intensity.

Several times a month, Jamie drives me to the emergency room. *I can't walk more than a few feet without being out of breath. I think I'm dying. I secretly wish I would.* We frequent new doctors' offices trying to find a diagnosis. Nothing shows up.

Anger continues to burn in my heart toward God.

You turned Your back and abandoned me. I decidedly turned mine on Him. *You are Almighty God! You could have prevented this!*

With the New Year comes a sense of panic and apprehension about the future although some things are marginally improving.

I feel that my marriage is ultimately in "destruction mode." I have to get a job as soon as possible. I have to become self-sufficient!

Daily, I comb through employment ads searching every possibility. I call some of them.

How on earth am I going to support myself and the kids?

That thought clings to my subconscious. Every time I try to figure out what to do next, God quietly whispers, "No...you don't need to look, you need to wait."

111

My new friend, Angel, shares about counseling she's undergoing. "Denise, you should go to a counselor."

"It's not going to happen. Forget it."

She doesn't mention it again. She goes to her sessions then comes home and shares with me things that help her. She suggests that I try part of her therapist's advice, "Why don't you consider telling Jamie that you're really struggling. Let him know that you can't continue your physical relationship as often as you did in the past. Let him know that you'll tell him a date that you'll be together intimately. Set the date often enough so that he doesn't feel mistreated, yet far enough apart that you don't feel used."

This works out well. Jamie is understanding and patient. He knows his infidelity led to our marriage problems. He wants our relationship to work. He's willing to do whatever's necessary.

On the Sundays that Jamie isn't working, he and the kids go to church. I attend occasionally. While there, my eyes probe the congregation longing for someone who might be able to tell me, "We've walked in your shoes. Our marriage survived." I never discover anyone who meets the qualification.

I'm still unable to look into anyone's eyes. One Sunday morning, a lady at church approaches me, "Would you be willing to teach a children's Sunday school class?" I shrug. "We need a teacher for the first grade, and I don't know if you could do this, but we have one child who's deaf who needs a class."

"I'll teach the deaf kid," I whisper.

"That'll be wonderful! Can you start next week if I get the material to you?"

I nod.

Good, I can lose myself in that. I won't have to go to Sunday school with Jamie. I hate being around groups of people. I feel everyone senses the coming collapse of our marriage.

God uses this avenue to get me to attend church weekly. Making sure our kids sit between Jamie and me, I even stay for the service.

A few Sundays later, our pastor preaches about the prodigal son. It's a good sermon. Then he speaks of the prodigal's brother's jealousy. He was angry about the Father's forgiveness.

God silently speaks to my heart. "You're acting exactly the same. You're angry with Me for forgiving Jamie."

You bet I'm angry! You forgive Your son, my husband's sin! It's not fair! Why does he get away with this?

Thoughts of betrayal and feelings of God pushing me aside course through my mind.

How could You abandon me? I'm the one who's faithful!

Suddenly I feel God's presence in my life. I know He didn't abandon me at all. He's been here all the time, hurting just as I hurt. Jamie's sin also causes Him pain. Yet my refusal for His comfort hurt Him as well. I eagerly go forward during the invitation, ready to ask God's forgiveness for turning my heart away from Him, ready to accept His love and healing. I rededicate my life to Him.

For the time being, I try to see Jamie as a parent would.

If he were my child, how would I react? How do I want my kid to be treated?

That helps some. Yet tension remains.

*****

At times, I still seethe with anger toward God. *This is so unfair! I didn't do anything wrong! I was a good wife! Why did you let this happen to me?*

God gently nudges my heart with His words, "Denise, do you remember the vision you had a few years ago? You were asked to come speak with Me in your living room. You didn't bother showing up."

But God! I was terrified! You are so holy! I'm so filthy!

"You would have been filthy without My son's blood covering your sins. Because you, my daughter, asked for My forgiveness, I see you as clean. Jamie, also My child, asked for my forgiveness. I provided it. He too is clean. I needed to show you that on your own, you're too sinful to come to Me. In exactly the same way, on his own, Jamie's too sinful. You each must come to Me to be cleansed. Only through Jesus can either of you approach Me. Neither of you can seek forgiveness for the other. It is an individual decision. I won't control Jamie, but neither do I control you. How close you and I are to each other is your choice."

Before He finishes speaking to my heart, tears stream down my face. *Yes, sir. I understand. Forgive my judgmental attitude. Let my relationship with You be better!*

*****

After another weary winter, I open my journal. The last entry I penned was in December. Today I write, "Lord, it's been a long time since I've written to You. I've just reread through this journal. What a crazy couple of years, huh? I feel as though I've traveled through most of it in a haze…probably Your protective covering over my emotions. Things are still rocky. I wish I knew if Jamie's truly repentant. He seems to have gone backward some. I feel weaker than this time last year, yet I'm still clinging to Your promises of restoration.

You've brought a dear friend into my life. I praise You for this blessing. Through her, You've helped sustain me. Lord, please continue to give me strength—spiritually, emotionally, and physically. Words from one of my favorite songs sung by Evie come to mind. 'I'm tired, I'm weak, and I'm worn—precious Lord, take my hand, lead me on, help me stand!' Please put Your loving arms around me and carry me a while longer. I love you, Lord!"[1]

Things at home are going a little better. I enjoy our new church. My sleeping marginally improves. One Sunday morning, God speaks to me through our pastor. "Denise, you need to readjust things in your home. There needs to be a balance between Jamie bending over backward to please you, and you being in charge. Ever since you found out about the affair Jamie's shown patience beyond description. He is humbly contrite."

I commit this to God. *Heavenly Father, I accept Jamie's repentance. Please restore proper authority in our home. If you put our marriage back together, I'll tell my story. I'll share what You did. But, Lord, I want our marriage to...more than just survive. If you choose to put the pieces back in place, I want it to thrive!*

Gradually I return the "reins" of leadership to Jamie. I eat every meal at the table with him and the kids. I do his laundry; dirty socks are still dirty socks, but I wash and fold them as though they're my own.

Once again, a hand gingerly grasps my neck.
Fingers tenderly hold me in place.
A chin nestles in my chin rest.
The bow slowly slides across my strings.
Interestingly, the music sounds better than before.
My mood changes from dread to anticipation.
Maybe there's hope yet.

14

Several months later, a smile lifts the corners of my lips as I glance out the window. The kids are in the backyard playing on their swing set. I hear Jamie enter our kitchen from the living room. He's carrying his Bible. "Denise, would you sit here with me?"

"Sure." After drying my hands, I sit on a bench across the table from him.

"Babe, for the past two and a half years you've asked me why I had the affair."

"Yeah."

Please don't rip the scab off!

"I haven't been able to answer because I didn't really know why I did it. I mean, I just did it. No thought about why."

"Yeah?"

"Well, I've been praying, reading my Bible, and asking God to show me why. This morning He did. He showed me. I was reading in James 1:13–15. Can I read it to you?"

"Sure," I curiously agree.

Jamie opens his Bible. "When tempted, no one should say, 'God is tempting me.' For God cannot be tempted by evil, nor does he tempt anyone; but each person is tempted when they are dragged away by their own evil desire and enticed. Then, after desire has conceived, it gives birth to sin; and sin, when it is full-grown, gives birth to death" (NIV).

Jamie's gaze lifts, his eyes lock with mine. "You see, that's where the problem started. I always thought it was okay to think about whatever came into my mind. I figured if you didn't know what I thought, it didn't matter. But by not controlling my thoughts, just like the verse says, I was 'dragged away by my own evil desire.' Once I allowed the thought to get comfortable in my mind is when it 'was conceived.' And once it was conceived, it 'gave birth to sin.' I'm not trying to oversimplify it, but God showed me I can't allow my mind to think about things that go against everything I know He's against."

"Okay."

"I asked God to help me control my thoughts, to help me not think the wrong things. Will you forgive me, not just for the affair, but also, for my thought life?"

My shoulders relax. "Yeah, baby, I will," I slide my hand across the table to grasp his.

Thank you, Lord, for speaking to Jamie. Thank you for changing his thought life. Thank You for this huge step!

I recall the counselor's words: "If you teach Jamie, it won't last... If God teaches him, it will last forever."

"Jamie, I think I need to talk to my folks. It's time to tell them."

"Okay. When are you going to do it?"

"While you're at work, I think we'll go up on Saturday."

"Okay." Jamie nods once while gently squeezing my hand. Then he leans across the table and kisses me.

Three days later, the kids and I visit my parents for the day. We eat lunch, and then the kids head out to play. "Dad, Mom, I need to talk to you."

"Okay." They shoot worried glances toward one another. "Let's go in the living room."

"I know you've been worried about me for the last several years. I need to tell you what's been going on." While I take a deep breath, Dad and Mom each seem to hold theirs.

"Jamie had an affair. He and I have been working through things. God's brought us through and taught us both a lot."

"Do you know who his mistress was?" Dad tenderly asks.

"Yes, Jamie confessed everything to me. At first, I was so angry! Gradually God turned that anger into grief, and then He gave me peace. Jamie's been extremely remorseful and apologetic. He's done everything

I've demanded. Recently he's gotten a word from God and is repentant. For the first time in a long time, I think we may stay together."

Mom gets up, comes to my side, gives me a tearful hug, and says, "I'm so sorry, Denise! Why didn't you tell us?"

"A counselor told me not to tell anyone."

"Do Jim and Terri know?"

"Yes. Jamie told them right after I found out."

"I'm proud of you, Denise," Dad lovingly states. "You have every right to leave him, but you stayed and let God work in and through you. I'm very proud of you," he repeats.

I relax into their sofa. "Thank you."

"Do the kids know?"

"No."

The five of us enjoy the rest of the day. I can tell a weight's lifted from Mom and Dad's shoulders as well. The kids and I return to our house before bedtime.

As our eleventh anniversary approaches, things between Jamie and me are pretty good.

I never would've believed it, but I even hope Jamie will ask me to renew our wedding vows!

Weeks pass.

He just doesn't "get it." He's oblivious to my hints.

Finally, as he looks over some bills, I share my wish. "Jamie, I'd like to renew our wedding vows."

His head shoots up as he whispers, "You'd be willing to do that? Even after all I've put you through?"

"Yes, baby, I am.

*****

Our pastor's wife approaches me at church the following month, "Denise, I'm having a lingerie party at my house Friday night after next. Here's your invitation." With a mischievous grin she adds, "There'll be about fifteen ladies from church! I hope you can make it!"

Our pastor's wife's throwing a lingerie party?

I blush. With a slight giggle, I reply, "I'll see if I can!"

I've got to call Angel when I get home!

"Angel, are you going to Maggie's party?"

"Of course! It'll be a blast! Suzie told me she's filling her van up with girls and will pick me…or us…up if you can make it. You're going, aren't you?"

"Just have to get someone to watch the kids."

"Mark will do it!" she giggles.

"Okay. I'll go!"

Twelve nights later, I walk across the street and ring Angel's doorbell. The two of us giggle, "Can you believe we're doing this?"

"Of course! It's going to be so fun!" She steps closer and nudges me, "You need to add some new spice in your life, girl! Oh look! Suzie's here!"

We scurry into the van where excited laughter greets us. Suzie, turning around in the driver's seat, interrupts, "Okay, girls. Here's your disguise!" She thrusts two small bags toward Angel and me, "Open them up! Hurry!"

We rip into the bags. Inside are rubber animal nose disguises! Angel and I look at each other then break out laughing.

"Here's the drill. When we get to Maggie's everyone put your mask on. That way no one will recognize us!" Suzie turns around and mashes the accelerator.

The party representative stands, "Thank you, Maggie, for hosting this party. Feel free to try on any, or all, of the inventory. Maggie has set up her bathrooms and bedrooms for dressing rooms. Here are catalogs. Have fun, gals!"

I choose several pieces. I slip into my favorite first. I smile as I look into the mirror.

I've got to buy this for our anniversary! I don't need to try the others on. This is it!

I redress and join Maggie and the representative in the living room.

"I'd like this one, please."

"Found one you like?" Blushing, I nod. "Oh, that's one of my favorites! Bet it looks beautiful on you!"

Angel rejoins us, holding her own favorites. I whisper as I lean toward her, "I'll wear this for our anniversary next week!"

"Jamie will love it!"

"I'll place your order and you'll get your items within the month.'

"Next month...but..."

"Yes, your order will be filled within the month. I'll deliver them to Maggie. She'll deliver them to their owners."

"But... I really want this tonight."

Angel emphatically voices her opinion, "Her anniversary is next week! She needs to take this home tonight!"

"Well, then, I have to sell this to her tonight!"

Angel and I are dropped off at her house after the party.

As I glance at my home, I notice the living room curtains are open; all the lights in the house are off.

Jamie's home and it looks like the kids are in bed.

Angel and I giggle but she comments first, "You've got to wear that home tonight!"

"That's what I was thinking, but I can't run across the street in a negligee!" Our snickers continue.

"I'll loan you my fur coat!"

"It's the end of July!"

"I know, but it's just across the street!"

I quickly change and don the fur. "See you tomorrow!"

"Have fun!"

Jamie glances in my direction as I enter the house. Noticing the fur, he inquires, "Did you wear that home?"

"Yes."

"How was the party?"

Closing the blinds, I pull him off the couch replying, "Great!"

*****

Our eleventh anniversary is a few days later; our pastor leads as we renew our vows. We invite very few people; Jim and Terri, Dad and Mom, our children, Angel and Mark her husband, and the pastor's wife.

Angel and Mark beautifully sing the duet titled, "Household of Faith," made popular by Steve Green.[2] Our pastor speaks, "Jamie, Denise, will you join me please?" We walk forward hand in hand.

"I will now lead Jamie and Denise in observing the Lord's Supper." Pastor Terry hands Jamie a matzo cracker, I grasp the other side. "The Lord's Supper is a celebration of God's grace. It is a sign of a relationship that is covenantal, not contractual. Jesus took the bread and said, 'This is My body given for you.'"

Together Jamie and I break the morsel. The snap reminds me of Jesus's broken body.

"Take, eat…"

Jamie and I swallow our portions. Pastor Terry hands Jamie a stoneware mug.

"Jesus said, 'This is my blood, take, drink…'"

We both drink the juice.

"Jamie and Denise will now renew their wedding vows. Jamie, please repeat after me…"

A gentle hand grasps my neck as warmth fills my chin rest.
A bow slides across the strings stretched over my core.
An elegant melody echoes from within my body.

15

That fall, John begins third grade, Shannon first. Angel's oldest daughter, Meaghan's in Shannon's class. Angel's hubby receives orders that he'll be transferred next spring. They have orders to move to another state.

Although life's much calmer, I still abhor living in this house. I can't wipe the thought that the "other woman" slept with my husband in this house from my mind. I still imagine that everyone I pass in the grocery store knows of Jamie's infidelity.

For our family to continue moving forward, change needs to happen.

A couple days after Christmas, I tell Jamie, "I want to start looking for another house after the first of the year."

"All right, we'll do that!" he excitedly agrees. Jamie understands that our history in this house keeps us anchored to the past.

I leave the next day to visit relatives for a few days. Three days later, I return home. I enter our kitchen. Greeting me with a hug, Jamie excitedly exclaims, "Great to see you! Guess what! The ad comes out in the paper tomorrow!"

"What? What ad?"

"You know…the ad to put our house on the market!"

"Oh, honey… I said after the first of the year!"

"Oh. Oh well. We may as well get this show on the road!"

"Okay." *Yikes!* Glancing around, my shoulders feel the monumental task's weight. I calculate as I scan our living room. The Christmas tree, still fully decorated, stands tall in all its glory.

Stockings still hang on the wall with care. Scattered torn bits of Christmas wrapping paper litter the corners.

Okey-dokey...time to get in overdrive!

John and Shannon, glad to be home, dart to and fro, "Where should I start?"

Well, I've already started in the garage.

Of course, where else would a man start!

"I think we should leave all the Christmas stuff in place. It makes things feel homier."

"All right, that's fine with me. Kids, come pick up your toys so I can vacuum!"

We get three offers on our house the next day! The first family hadn't prequalified so we move forward with the next two. The second offer backs out. The third is a single man who works in construction. He comes over that evening and signs the contract.

The next week I answer a phone call, "Mrs. Royal?"

"Yes."

"The bank says your house is overpriced and won't loan me the money for the full amount. Would it be okay if I sign a paper stating I still want the house? I've got the rest in my savings account. Can I just write you a check for that amount?"

"That's fine as long as it's a cashier's check."

"Great! It looks like everything is a go!"

"Great! Do we have a closing date yet?"

"Yep, it's six weeks from today!"

Six weeks! Yikes! I better kick the packing into high gear! Lord, please provide our next house ASAP!

Between packing and looking at houses, I hardly have a moment's rest. Jamie and I look at homes together at first. We go see a house. Driving to the location, Jamie declares, "It's got a two-car garage." Then we go inside. Jamie's next stop is the garage to see if the property has a sprinkler system. "Yep, it has a sprinkler system." Those two items make up his list of requirements. I wander from room to room.

Every bedroom is on different floors?

At the next house, Jamie's remarks are the same.

This house has all the bedrooms on the same floor, but why is the kitchen crammed far away from all the other rooms? I won't even be able to see the kids! The backyard is tiny!

This scenario plays over and over. Days tick by. Fed up, Jamie proclaims, "That's it. I'm through looking. When you find something, let me know."

"Okay."

Yeah! That clears me to look while he's at work! We won't be arguing over details!

That evening, after Jamie goes to work and the kids are in bed, I continue packing our clothes. I reach into the bottom drawer of my dresser vanity. My fingers feel paper under my lingerie. I pull the drawer out and dump all the contents on the floor in front of me. A small envelope catches my eye as I sit Indian-style on the carpet.

Hm, what's this? It can't be... I forgot all about this commitment card from the women's retreat! I can't even remember what God asked me to write down.

Slowly I unseal the envelope. There's my commitment card stating, "Lord, help me love Jamie unconditionally."

Wow! Lord, You had everything lined up, didn't You? Thank You! You're incredible!

When Jamie gets home, I meet him at the door. "Honey, you're not going to believe this!

Look! See what I wrote to God a few months before I found out about your affair?"

Jamie glances at the commitment card. Tears fill his eyes as he reads it.

Humbly, he replies, "That's amazing. Thank you for showing it to me." He tenderly hugs me.

We "subscribe" to a weekly flier advertising homes for sale by their owners. The first few weeks bring few choices. The next week, I misplace the paper. I call the company's office, "Could you resend the ad? I've lost mine."

"We certainly will. I'll stick it in the mail today!" It arrives in my mailbox two mornings later, a day earlier than anyone else is due to get the next week's flier. There's a new listing. I call the phone number but get no answer.

"Honey, I know you're tired of looking at houses, but this one sounds really interesting. Can we drive by and at least see if we like the neighborhood?"

"I don't see why not! Kids! Get in the car! We're going for a ride!"

I'm a little concerned about the house being on such a hilly road, but the house is beautiful! Jamie parks the car in the driveway. "I'll just go to the door and see if anyone is home." He strides to the front door then returns. "There's no one home." As he starts to get back in the car, a neighbor walks toward our vehicle.

"Can I help you?"

"Oh, we just want to look at the house."

"Well, I live next door. I can't show you inside, but I know the owners wouldn't mind if you see the backyard!"

"Okay! That sounds great! Denise, kids, come see the backyard!"

The three of us pile out. We follow Jamie and the neighbor through the fence. We walk the length of the garage. Once we turn the corner Jamie's and my mouths drop open. We're greeted by a spacious yard overlooking an uninhibited view of Pike's Peak! "We've got to see this place!" Jamie exclaims. "Let's go home, grab some lunch, and retry to contact the owners!"

Over lunch, Jamie openly ponders, "Wonder why the house is priced so low. Other houses in that neighborhood are at least $10,000 more."

He calls the owners after finishing his sandwich. "They're home! We can see the house as soon as we can get there!"

We pile back into the car. I push one of the kids' favorite cassettes into the car stereo. The song "I Expect a Miracle" begins playing.[3] We all laugh excitedly! We play and replay that song the whole way. United, we sing the lyrics with enthusiastic joy. "I anticipate the inevitable supernatural intervention of God! I expect a miracle!"

Arriving at the destination, we eagerly approach the front door. Jamie knocks as only a police officer would; using the side of his fist. The owners greet us warmly and invite us inside. Jamie and I glance at each other as a spacious entryway envelops us. Light oak banisters lead both upstairs and down. The couple parades us throughout the house, each room perfectly delightful.

The tour complete, Jamie and I nod toward each other. Jamie inquires, "Can we sit down and talk with you?"

"Sure. Let's go into the dining room."

"Why are you selling?"

"Well, we've lived here two and a half years. We never lived in a city before. My wife's afraid here. We want to go back to the country."

"We'd like to make an offer."

The woman's mouth drops. "What?"

"We'd like to make an offer," Jamie repeats.

"B...bu...but I'm not ready to sell yet!" the lady squeaks out.

"Well, the ad is official, isn't it?" Jamie continues.

The husband answers, "Yes, we just thought it would probably take several months."

We agree on the price almost instantaneously. The man walks out of the room and returns with the contract for us to sign.

Later, Jamie calls the buyer for our current house, "Hi, Jamie Royal here. I hate to ask this but we just found our next home. Is there any way we could rent our house until we are able to close on the next one?"

"That won't be a problem. I'll see you at the closing. Your rent will be whatever your current mortgage payment on this house is."

"It's a deal! See you at the closing!"

After closing on our new home, we move all our items there. Jamie drives our family back to the old place for one last time to do one last thorough cleaning. Jamie goes over the yard, and then he checks the garage and shed for forgotten items. I vacuum and wipe things off. I pour strong cleanser into warm water in the kitchen sink. With rag in hand, I wipe out every kitchen cabinet. Squatting,

I scrub the lower ones. I pull the vacuum cleaner closer as I slide open the "bread" drawer.

This drawer's always full of bread crumbs, chip bits, and twist ties. I'll just grab the ties, vacuum up the crumbs, and then wipe it out.

Ready for the task, a shiny object stuck in the far-left corner of the drawer catches my eye. *That girl gets her stuff everywhere. Looks like one of Shannon's sequins made it in here.* Smiling, I shake my head. *Shannon likes crafts more than anything else we give her.* A subtle thought pops into my mind. *Knock it out of place before vacuuming the drawer.*

I flick the object with my fingernail hoping to dislodge it. I dislodge it all right! Out jumps my engagement diamond! I squeal and jump to my feet. "Jamie! Kids! Come 'ere!" I run toward Jamie, "Honey! Look! God gave my diamond back! Look!" I extend my hand palm up revealing the precious stone. Making a fist to secure the diamond, I wrap my arms around him as we kiss deeply. The kids charge toward us to see why I'm making such a fuss. Happy to see their parents' excitement, the four of us meld into one laughing, crying huddle. *You're putting it all back together! Thank You! Thank You, Lord!*

Somehow, when hearing the symphony,
all forget all the labor required to make the concert happen.
We stroll away, full of hope and promise, humming.
Our hearts remember only the beautiful melody.

SYMPHONY MOVEMENT NO. 2

Rehearsals

16

My closest friend's husband, Mark, gets orders to be stationed at another Army base. Therefore, a week after we move into our new home, Angel and her family move in with us for their final week in Colorado. Through hugs and tears, we say our goodbyes.

Lord, what'll I do without her? I'll probably never see her again. After all, why would I? Throughout my life, when someone moves, that's the end of our relationship. Move on, get over it.

My kids finish the last nine weeks of the school year at their new elementary school. Although John misses his friends, he says the new school is "okay." Shannon's teacher is completely the opposite from the one who previously taught her. Although my girl struggles making new friends at school, she gets along all right with our neighbor's girls. We also change churches to one closer to our new home.

As we meet several members at our new church home, Jamie mentions, "Why don't we have someone over for dinner? Just seeing people at church isn't enough to get to know them."

"Good idea! Who should we start with?"

"How about the couple whose daughter goes to school with John? They must live in our neighborhood."

Jamie invites them to come to our place for dinner the following week. Moments before our company is to arrive, Shannon sneaks around the kitchen door and blasts Jamie with Silly String. He chases her, grabs the can, and unleashes its contents.

"You two cut it out! Curt and Alta will be here any minute!"

Jamie's gaze returns to Shannon and then both grin as their eyes turn to me. *Uh-oh! I should've kept my mouth shut!* I squeal as Jamie runs to catch me. One arm envelops me, the other hand pulls the back of my pants. I feel the gross slime squirt down my jeans as the doorbell rings.

"You two answer the door! I've got to clean myself up!"

Curt, Alta, and their daughter, Jana, enter the living room as I exit the bathroom. Shannon's excitement overflows, "Dad just squirted Silly String down Mom's pants!"

So much for trying to look like the perfect Christian family! Laughter fills the room.

We also make friends in our new neighborhood. One woman and I get together at least once every six weeks. At one of our gatherings, she breaks into tears, "I think I'm still in love with my ex-husband! Years ago, he left me for another woman. When he later asked me to come back to him, I refused. Now, he's marrying someone else!"

Hugging her, I admit, "I understand some of your pain."

"How could you?"

"We don't tell many people, but years ago, Jamie had an affair."

"And you stayed with him?"

"Yes."

She cries harder. "I didn't know that was an option!"

That evening I share the event with Jamie. He replies, "We've got to let people know that God can do the impossible!"

My health and lack of strength remain a challenge. We continue seeking a medical answer.

Something has to be wrong! The chest pains must be caused by something! We see one doctor after another. Each orders a wide array of tests… blood work, stress test, EKG, ultrasounds. No one can find my problem.

This continues for over a year after our move. One night God speaks to me in a dream. I write in my journal, "Praise You, Lord for speaking to me last night! Surely it was Your hand that touched me and restored me spiritually and emotionally! A heavy weight's gone! I praise You, Lord! Communication with You is restored! The emotional damage of the last two and a half years was healed—all in a split second! You spoke and reminded me of Your promise in 1 Peter 5:10b (NIV): "After you have suffered a little while, (God) will Himself restore you and make you strong, firm, and steadfast." You did it, Lord! You restored me. You said, "It's been enough. Your suffering has ended." Praise You! You are a loving and compassionate God. Forgive my defiance against You. Forgive me for not accepting Your grace. Forgive me for not trusting You."

The news bursts out as soon as Jamie wakes, "Honey, God healed me last night! He told me that I've suffered enough!" That day, our family goes to church, enjoys a home-cooked meal, and I still feel energetic!

"Let's go for a walk around the block! We haven't done that in at least a year!"

Halfway, Jamie lovingly questions, "You still okay? Do you need to rest?"

"I'm great! God healed me, babe! He told me this morning I was healed! The chest pain was all because of my rebellion against Him. He told me, 'It's been enough.' The chest pains are over! I feel wonderful! I have more energy than I've had in years! God healed my heart!"

Jamie's arms engulf me in a bear hug. He picks me up off the ground and swings me around.

We quickly locate a church near our new home. Little by little, though, Jamie starts missing church again.

Church brothers and sisters ask, "Is Jamie sick?"

"No. He just didn't want to come."

I'm not going to lie for him like I used to.

"I'm sorry, I'll pray for him."

"Thanks." *That feels so much better. It's not my burden; it's between Jamie and God.*

Several months later, a church brother approaches me. "We're having a men's retreat! I'm going to call Jamie and invite him!"

"Thanks!"

Doubt he'll go, but thanks!

Later that week, Jamie receives a phone call. I casually listen.

"Hi, Dave! How ya doing? Yeah, me too. Life stays busy. My job? It's good. Got into quite a scuffle last week!" Pause. "Really, next weekend? Huh, I'll see what I can do. Thanks for calling! Bye."

"That was Dave. He told me there's a men's thing at the church Friday night through Saturday afternoon. Told him I might go. Do we have any plans?"

"None that I know of."

"Hmm, I guess I could go Friday night for a while. Doubt I'll go Saturday."

"Okay." *Thank You, Lord!*

Friday after work, Jamie comes home, grabs his Bible, and heads out for the evening. "See you later, baby! Love you!"

"Love you too!" *Lord, be with him!*

Jamie calls around ten thirty. "Hi, babe. I'm going to stay the night. I decided to stay through tomorrow afternoon."

"That's fine. Thanks for letting me know. Love you!"

"Love you too! Night!"

Lord, I trust that You're working. Please have him be at the church! Please speak to him!

Jamie arrives home Saturday evening; when I meet him at the door, he's crying.

"What's up, babe?"

"Oh, Denise, God's doing such a work in my life! I'm a changed man! I know I asked Jesus into my life when I was a teenager, but I never gave Him control until this morning!"

*****

A few years later, Jamie arrives home from work with big news, "I'm moving into investigations. I start Monday."

"Awesome! Why aren't you more excited?"

"I'm assigned to juvenile sex crimes."

"Oh. I'm sorry."

Lord, be with him. You know how tender-hearted he is toward children!

Monday afternoon, I meet Jamie as he comes in our door. I cautiously question, "Hi, babe, how was your day?"

Jamie grabs me in one arm and exclaims, "Great! You're not going to believe this… I go into the juvenile sex crimes office this morning and everyone says, 'What're you doing here?' I tell them I'm assigned here. They say, 'You didn't hear? Another detective wants this position. You're in auto theft!'"

"Oh, honey! I'm so glad! I was worried about the other position!"

"And get this… I don't have to wear a suit—just jeans and tennis shoes!"

Thank You, Lord! A perfect fit for my man!

Jamie excels in his new job. He grows in knowledge and respect. God opens my eyes. "I do want Jamie on the police department."

But Lord, what about the dream?

"Don't worry about that. Jamie is where I want him for now."

Our pastor begins a new class on Sunday nights called "Experiencing God."[4] Jamie and I attend. Through this course, our spiritual lives become vibrant. We learn that God is always at work around us, how to recognize His activity, and to be prepared for His invitation to join Him where He's moving. This invitation often leads to a crisis of faith that requires action. If we choose to join Him, we experience Him in unimaginable ways. We lead several groups through this material anytime we get the chance.

*****

Several years later, I trip over something behind me. Instinctively, I catch myself. Intense pain courses up both arms. *Umph!*

Jamie asks, "You okay?"

"Don't know, think I broke my wrists."

"Oh, baby! I'll take you in to get checked out."

The X-rays don't show any breaks. My general practice doctor sends me to physical therapy and an orthopedist. Jamie takes John, now fifteen, to the Department of Motor Vehicles to get him a special permit to allow him to drive me to doctor appointments. John's overjoyed!

At the first appointment to which he drives me, the doctor orders steroid injections. Mistakenly, I allow John to follow me into the examination room.

John's eyes open widely when the nurse enters with two syringes. Each have one-a-half-inch needles.

Don't let him see my fear or pain!

The treatment provides no relief.

Great! Now I'm stuck at home, can't cook, clean, read, hold the TV remote, brush my hair or teeth. Way to go, Grace!

A friend gives me a book by Anne Graham Lotz, "The Vision of His Glory."[5] Although its theme is the book of Revelation, God opens my eyes to the Apostle John's possible perspective. He was in the middle of active ministry when thrown into prison. As if that wasn't bad enough, he's exiled to the island of Patmos!

Thank You, God, for showing me that if John hadn't been sent to Patmos, we wouldn't have the book of Revelation! Although I'm limited by what I can see, You see the entire picture. I trust that You know what You're doing!

Boredom allows me to remember a video series my in-laws loaned me two years ago. My attitude stunk when Terri first brought them to me. *Great! What does she think I need to know?*

The videos, "The Life" by Bill and Anabel Gillham, teach spiritual truths in ways I've never understood.[6] They share that "the Christian life isn't difficult to live, it's impossible! Jesus Christ is the only one who has ever really lived the Christian life, and He's the only one who can live it today, and He wants to do it in and through me!" They teach how God's love for me isn't based on what I do but simply on the fact that I am His child! I also learn the Christian life isn't something I'm going to do in the future. I am to let Christ live through me today. Bill Gillham shares, "This life is our only chance to live by faith."

The following January, while teaching a craft class to elementary home-school children, I lose my left field of vision. After class I call to one of the helpers, "Honey, please go to the office and ask one of the teachers to come." My friend comes within a few minutes. "I don't know what's wrong, but I can't see the left side of anything with either eye. I'm gonna need someone to drive me home." Once home, I rest. My vision's fine when I wake up the next morning.

Jamie voices his concern, "Think you should see the doctor. Let him check things out and make sure you're okay."

"But I feel fine today."

"Good, but please get an appointment anyway."

Our doctor's receptionist makes an appointment for the next week.

My doc reviews my last year's records, examines my eyes, and has me do some minor exercises. "Denise, are you feeling all right? Any other concerns?"

"Just normal stuff, tired, headache, but that's normal."

"Okay, I don't see anything right off the bat, but I'm giving you orders to have an MRI. Make a follow-up appointment two weeks after it's done."

Several weeks later, I reappear in his clinic. As he enters with my chart in his hands, his brow furrows. "Hi, Denise. It's good to see you again."

"You too, Doc."

His eyes tear up as he studies my chart. He clears his throat, "Denise, I'm afraid your MRI shows you probably have MS, multiple sclerosis."

God's peace blankets me. "It's okay, sir. God will take care of me. I'll be fine."

"I'm referring you to a neurologist, and I'd like to see you again after your appointment."

"Thank you. I'll be fine, sir."

John and Shannon teach at our church tonight so I wait until they leave our house to talk to Jamie. "My MRI shows I might have multiple sclerosis."

"I'm not even sure what that is! What do you know about it?"

"Well, it's a disease that affects the nerve linings in a person's brain. Symptoms depend on where the nerve linings are."

"Is it fatal?"

"Not sure. Think I might end up in a wheelchair."

"I'll be with you no matter what!" He hugs me tightly then prays, "Lord, we don't know what we're facing, but You do. Be with us. Guide us. Heal Denise if it's Your will!"

We tell the kids when they return home later. Their eyes cloud with tears as they ponder the unknown. John replies, "I'll do whatever I need to do!" Shannon nods.

The only thing similar to what I went through during our marriage trials is the exhaustion. Thank You, Lord, that I'm not having the chest pain!

The Conductor, knowing each musician and instrument personally, places each in their proper place.
We work in seamless unity.

17

Shannon starts having horrendous abdominal pain eighteen months later. Some of our friends speculate "she's stressed" over me or "having sympathetic pains." After many weeks, doctors suggest it must be her gallbladder. Jamie and I reluctantly give permission for its removal.

Within six months her pain's back. At first, it's only once or twice a month and then weekly, now daily. Nothing ever shows up on the medical tests. Day after day she sits bent at the waist on our couch, rocking back and forth continually. Her face is pale and drawn, her lips dry. Throwing up becomes so common for her, I stop counting its frequency.

Today she's worse than ever. She and I get into our car for another day in the emergency room. The Emergency Room staff glances up as we enter. Eyebrows raise, and then all eyes return to their desks.

"Hi, we're back."

"All right, ma'am, just fill out the forms. Take a seat."

"I'll need a vomit bag."

"Here you go."

I take the form; write the same information I gave yesterday. After handing Shannon the bag, I sit next to her as she continues rocking. After a couple of hours, we're called back to an examination room. Today's doctor enters, glances at Shannon as he shakes his head, "We gave you pain medicine last time you were here. Now you're back again."

Shannon doesn't bother looking at the man.

"We're here because she isn't any better. Something has to be wrong."

"Draw some more blood." Shannon's arms are black and blue from previous blood draws. "I'll be back when we get the results."

"Do you need anything?" the nurse asks before leaving the room.

Shannon weakly states, "A warm blanket please."

The doctor reenters thirty minutes later. "The tests are normal. You're released."

Shannon and I wearily depart.

We see our family doctor again the next morning. His eyes tear up. Shannon babysat his two daughters when she was healthier. "I'm trying to get you into another GI doctor. I'm so sorry Shannon! I wish there was more I could do! You've seen every specialist I've recommended. The internal medicine doctor's puzzled as well. Go to the emergency room if your pain is more than you can stand, although you're taking too much medicine already."

I drive straight to the ER. *Second verse, same as the first.* Today we see a different doctor, Dr. Tietz. He reads her chart and orders the same tests.

As we wait for the results, I call a church friend, Mark Campbell, an air force doctor. He knows our family well. Shannon also occasionally babysat his daughter. I know this is a crucial week in his career. He's preparing for upcoming tests. I explain Shannon's symptoms.

"Ask the doctor to have her amylase and lipase levels checked. Sounds like pancreatitis."

Upon Dr. Tietz's return, I ask, "Would you please check her amylase and lipase levels?" His eyebrows rise slightly.

"Sure. Nurse, please draw blood for more tests. This will take at least an hour to get the results. I'll be back when they come in.

"Thank you, sir." Shannon and I wait. She continues rocking. She no longer cries out in pain. Now her screams are eerily silent, as though she has no vocal cords.

Finally, the doctor appears reading the paperwork. "My God! This child has pancreatitis! Get her some pain medicine ASAP!" Nurses flurry into activity. "We are admitting her immediately."

The next several years creep in slow motion. Often after emergency room visits, doctor appointments, or hospitalizations Jamie and I collapse into bed. Both of us needing to be held and loved, we escape into each other's embrace. Our world's upside-down but let our guard down with each other. Being vulnerable we pray, cry, and lean upon each other.

Thank You, God! You got us through another day.

The monotonous daily crises leave us mentally and emotionally exhausted. My mind goes into an automatic mind-numbed state.

After multiple hospital stays, doctors call us into a conference room. "Mr. and Mrs. Royal, we recommend putting a Groshong tube into Shannon's chest. This will make drawing blood and giving medication easier."

The doctors explain the procedure thoroughly. We consent. They take our daughter into surgery to implant this device. Tears distort my vision when she comes out of the recovery room.

Lord, this seems so…so…permanent! Is this going to be her life from now on?

They release her from the hospital a few days later. By this point, Shannon's being fed intravenously. The amount of pain medicine she's prescribed could kill the average person. Each morning I whisper a silent prayer. *God, help Shannon be alive. Help me as I go downstairs to check on her.* Steadying myself, I inhale deeply before entering her room.

Is she still breathing?

More and more, she begins sleeping on our bedroom floor as the medications cause horrendous nightmares.

Lord, this all seems so useless! I don't understand why You're not healing her! Please help!

A couple times each year, the MS flares up affecting my vision, giving me severe headaches, and/or stiffening my left leg muscles so

I can barely walk. My neurologist orders IV steroids to be administered at home.

Jamie does all he can to help at me home. If the sink is full of dirty dishes, he washes them; laundry not done? He throws a load in the washer.

John also chips in with both house and yardwork. He sits by his sister's side whenever she's hospitalized.

To assist in answering repeated questions about both Shannon and my health issues, Jamie and I keep notes recording symptoms, meds taken and lab results.

By August 2001, Shannon's pancreatitis is worse than ever. She's admitted to the city hospital yet again. She's listed as NPO, (no food by mouth) again, meaning she can neither eat nor drink until the pancreas settles down. Jamie and I take turns sitting with her around the clock. After two weeks, nothing has changed. Her enzyme levels are exactly the same. She loses weight daily.

"You have her statistics written down?" the doctors question. "You two seem like helicopter parents."

"She's with you all the time?"

"Does Shannon get out of the house with friends?"

Each hospital worker seems to ask the same questions. They use different wording maybe, but the same tone with the same raised eyebrows.

What part of "She's too sick to get out of bed," do you not understand?

She is in the hospital two weeks when Jamie demands, "We want her transferred to Denver to the University of Colorado Children's Hospital."

"I believe we can handle this here. There's no need to transfer her."

"We've waited fourteen days. You've accomplished nothing!"

"Sir...with pancreatitis, these things can take time."

"We know. This isn't her first case of pancreatitis! The other day I had to tell a nurse that she wasn't getting enough fluids to keep her alive! The nurse checked, and sure enough, I was right! The machine was on the wrong setting! Have her transferred!"

"I believe she needs to be seen by a psychiatrist."

"You've mentioned that before but no one has come by to see her!"

"I'll work on it," he states as he turns and leaves the room.

"This is ridiculous!" Exasperated, Jamie turns to face me. We hold one another as Shannon continues rocking from the relentless pain. Her cries are silent. Her face contorts with pain. With tears streaming down her face, her mouth opens as if to scream, but still no sound escapes.

I visit the head nurse again, stating, "I want to contact social services."

"Why? What's going on?"

"Well, if my daughter was at home and I refused to give her the proper care, you could call social services and report child neglect. We've been here over two weeks. You have neglected to administer TPN, (intravenous food), proper hydration, and are refusing to move her to Denver. I believe that qualifies as child neglect."

"Ma'am, I believe you're overreacting."

"The doctor told us again two days ago that a psychiatrist would be by to evaluate her. No one's been by."

"Well… I'll check on that."

"I want you to call social services or I will."

"Ma'am…let me talk to your doctor. I'll get back to you as soon as possible!"

"The clock is ticking!" I spit out before leaving her office.

Within the hour a psychiatrist comes to question Shannon. "Mrs. Royal, I need your permission to speak with your daughter."

"Go ahead."

She stays in Shannon's room about forty-five minutes. I sit at the end of the hall in the waiting area. I watch the doctor exit Shannon's room and gently close the door. Nodding in my direction, she walks the long hallway then sits next to me. "Mrs. Royal, I believe Shannon may have some kind of eating disorder."

"Why is that?"

"Well, she seems to associate food with pain."

"Mm-hm. What I am curious about is, how can she control her pancreatic enzyme levels with her mind?"

"What do you mean?"

"Well, if you'll look at her medical charts, you'll see that every time she's been admitted her lab work shows she has pancreatitis. How does she do that if it is only a psychological problem?"

The young doctor looks flustered. "Let me check on that and get back to you."

Within ninety minutes, paperwork's printed off, forms signed, and an ambulance is on its way to take Shannon to Denver.

Jamie calls the Denver Ronald McDonald House. "Hi, this is Jamie Royal. My seventeen-year-old daughter is being transferred from Memorial Hospital in Colorado Springs to Children's Hospital. Do you have a room available that my wife and I can rent?"

"Yes, a room was vacated earlier today."

"We'll take it."

Jamie and I follow the ambulance in our personal vehicle to Children's Hospital. He lets me out at the door where the paramedics are unloading Shannon. I follow them into the hospital and onto the elevator. The doors part and they wheel her toward a locked door. My gaze shoots up to the sign overhead, "PSYCHIATRIC AREA. Ring bell for assistance." The paramedic pushes the button.

Lord, no way! They can't be putting her in the psych ward!

"Can I help you?" a stale voice asks through the speaker.

"Yes. We've got Shannon Royal here. She's been transferred from Memorial Hospital in Colorado Springs."

"Shannon Royal? We weren't alerted of her arrival."

"Yes. We were told to bring her to this ward. She has chronic pancreatitis."

"I'm afraid you have the wrong floor. You need to be on the fourth floor."

My shoulders relax. I discard the unspoken arguments my mind prepared.

Shannon's placed in her assigned room. Jamie and I begin unpacking her things. The normal hustle and bustle of hospital

144

admissions swamps the room. Paperwork completed. Check. ID bracelet placed on Shannon's wrist. Check. Shannon reconnected to IV fluids. Check.

A nurse assistant arrives. "Hi, my name is Andrea. I'll be your medical assistant today," her young voice chirps. "This is the nurse call button. Here's your TV remote control. You get several channels and also, we have a video library. This is the menu…oops! You're TPN! You're not allowed to eat or drink anything. Sorry! Let me get your weight, temp, and blood pressure."

"Okay, you're all set. Your nurse and doctor will be in soon. If you need anything, just push the call button. I'll be back in a little while."

"Ma'am?" I interject.

"Yes?"

"We need some vomit bags."

"Oh! Of course, I'll run and get them!"

Jamie and I wearily sit on the room's love seat. I finally take a deep breath. We slide closer together. With sighs of relief, we lean against one another.

The momentary stillness is interrupted by reality. "Dad?" Shannon whispers.

"Right here, Sweetie," he stands as he speaks. He grasps her tiny, weak hand. "What can I do for you?"

She points at her mouth.

Jamie shouts, "Oh! Grab the trash can!"

I jump to my feet and place the bin in front of her just before the eruption.

"Sorry. Thanks, Mom."

"Honey, it's not a problem. I should have been ready."

Just then the medical assistant arrives. "I'm sorry! I tried to hurry!"

"You're fine. Thank you," Jamie replies.

A few minutes later, a middle-aged woman enters our "humble abode." She lifts Shannon's wrist to check the ID bracelet. "Hi, my name is Karen. I'll be your nurse for the rest of the day. Let's see. Yes. I've got your meds. Let me put them in your IV."

Another middle-aged woman enters. This one's wearing a suit. She's reading Shannon's chart. "I'm Dr. Jones. Mm-hm. I see you've got pancreatitis. Well, I don't know what we can do differently for you here than what the Colorado Springs hospital was doing. The orders are the same: TPN, same medications. All right. Well, you'll just have to wait the pancreatitis out. If it doesn't get better, we can remove your pancreas and you'll live for a little while. Then you'll die." Shannon bursts into tears. The doctor then abruptly turns and exits.

Jamie follows her out. "Ma'am, I don't see any reason for your rudeness."

"And who are you?"

"I'm Shannon's Dad."

"Well, sir. I don't know how things are done in Colorado Springs but here we don't sugarcoat the truth."

Jamie, frustrated to a breaking point, walks away.

The Ronald McDonald House is just across the street. We walk to our luxurious room every evening, and then retrace the route the following morning.

Thank You for a place to stay and for the gracious people who provide for caregivers! They've thought of everything: laundry facilities, a kitchen, large dining room, playground for young children, even snacks!

Jamie has enough sick time at work saved to be able to be with us. Other officers even want to donate time if his runs out.

John starts college and watches over our home.

I hate that I'm not able to fuss over him! John's stood by Shannon's side whenever possible. Thank You, Lord, for that young man!

*The orchestra continues relentless practice.
I whine, "Really, Sir? I'm going to be
worn out before we ever perform!"*

18

Shannon's pancreatitis doesn't improve. One night, after Jamie and I trudge back from the hospital, we collapse on the bed immediately. The phone rings as I start to doze off.

Jamie answers, "Hello. Okay. We'll be right there."

"What's going on?"

"Shannon said we need to come back immediately."

"All right, let's get going."

Once back in the hospital, we take the elevator to Shannon's floor. The door opens; we step out and walk around the corner to the hallway leading to her room.

Lord! There's a bright light coming from her room! What's happening?

Our pace quickens as we grab each other's hand. Nurses barely glance up as we whisk past their station.

The closer we get to Shannon's room the brighter the light glows. My first glimpse of Shannon steals my breath.

She's lying on her back perfectly still. The light I saw is coming from her face! She's as white as the sheet on which she lays.

Lord, I don't remember when she's been so still and able to lay on her back.

Peace engulfs us as we enter her room. All fear is gone.

Jamie speaks first, "We're here, honey."

Her eyes open. Her voice is quiet as a whisper. "Thanks for coming."

"What's going on, honey?"

Calmly and peacefully, she answers, "God told me I'm going to die."

"We're here for you, we love you."

"God told me I'm going to die…tonight."

Breathe…breathe… Lord, help us!

Again, Jamie replies first, "We love you! I don't think you're going to die tonight." His eyes brim with tears.

We both hold her hands.

Finally, I find my voice, "Shannon, God may have told you that, but I'm praying for Him to extend your life."

Jamie leads us in prayer then, wordlessly, he and I turn and walk back to our room, cocooned in otherworldly peace.

Lord, I don't understand what You're doing!

"It's not about you."

Unimaginable peace allows Jamie and me to get a full night's sleep.

The following morning, Shannon's back to her rocking behavior. She speaks as we enter, "I'm embarrassed about last night. God told me I was going to die, but I'm still here!"

Embracing her I utter, "Don't be embarrassed. We prayed for God to extend your life and He did! We're glad you called!"

A couple of weeks later, her pancreatic enzyme levels slowly lower enough for her to be discharged. Jamie picks us up at the hospital's front door.

He exclaims as he helps our daughter into the back seat, "Free at last, Shannon!"

"The fresh air feels great!"

Our girl sleeps most of the way home. Jamie and I, physically and emotionally spent, are quiet.

Lord, Thank You for extending Shannon's life, but now what? She's still so sick! Guide us and heal our girl!

At her next appointment, one doctor suggests possible sphincter of Oddi dysfunction. "She can have surgery to cut that muscle."

Neither Jamie nor I have peace about the suggested surgery that would cut the muscle from an "O" form into a "C" form. We'd heard this often causes unstoppable diarrhea.

Shannon quickly bounces back and staying true to her routine, has a job within a month. Child care work energizes her. Daycare centers recognize her giftedness; therefore, she's frequently moved to the toughest centers until things level out. Then, she's transferred to another challenge. She works with babies through high schoolers. Her specialty is troubled children and those with special needs.

Several months pass, then she's back in the hospital with pancreatitis, again.

Lord, stop this crazy ride! I want to get off!

*****

A couple of years after the Children's Hospital experience, Shannon approaches Jamie and me. "I want to go to drug rehab. I'm tired of not remembering my life."

Jamie answers, "We appreciate you wanting to get off the painkillers, but the doctors have said you'll never be able to live without them."

"But Dad, I'm serious. I've given this a lot of thought. I want to get off them!"

"I'll look into our insurance and see what it provides."

Several nights later, Jamie informs us, "Shannon, our insurance will pay for you to go to a local drug rehab program. You can check in next Monday."

Jamie drives the three of us to the institution several days later. He leads in prayer before we exit the car. "You're sure this is what you want?"

"Yes, Dad."

"Okay, then, let's go."

The charge nurse meets with us. "You won't be able to talk to Shannon until next weekend. Then you can visit Saturday and Sunday from one to three."

Lord, be with her! These people look like someone Jamie arrests!

I feel like we're living in a different reality.

Is this all just a horrible nightmare? God, do you hear? Why're You letting her go through this? It is so hard to watch my child suffer!

I hear a tender Voice speak to my heart, "I know. I watched My child suffer, for you. I could have stopped it but I didn't. I allowed His pain and death for you."

Lord, You're right! You do understand!

Our friends and church family continue to pray for us.

An unexpected bill from the rehab center shows up in our mail today for $837. The notice demands immediate payment.

Lord, we don't have spare money!

Jamie and I manage to scrape the money together.

Less than ten days later, my dentist's office calls, "Mrs. Royal?"

"Yes."

"Remember last year when you got your mouthpiece?"

"Mm-hm."

"Well, we rebilled your insurance and they paid 100 percent! We've got a $824 check for you!"

Thank You, Lord, for supplying the funds for last week's crisis!

Shannon comes home from the program a completely different woman. Her eyes and mind are clear. Rehab taught Shannon she was not "chemically dependent" on the narcotics as doctors told us, but she is an addict. They encouraged her to join a Narcotics Anonymous group as soon as possible.

Jamie voices our concern, "Shannon, you're not the same as addicts. You didn't choose to take drugs!"

"Dad, I am an addict. I want to stay clean and the meeting will help me."

"I'm concerned about the men you'll meet. Promise me you won't date any of them!"

"I'm not planning on going to the meetings to meet guys! Geez, Dad!"

A year later Shannon announces, "I'm getting my one-year chip at next week's meeting! You're invited!"

Anger wells up in my heart. *Lord, she's not an addict!*

"I won't be there."

Jamie interjects, "I will."

"Thank you, Dad. Mom, you're invited if you decide to come."

Six days later, guilt takes over as Jamie gets ready for the meeting. "I still don't agree with this whole Narcotics Anonymous deal, but I guess I'll go."

The small room is fairly full. Many are clearly addicts; some not as obvious. Family and friends sit by most of the members. Each "addict" shares their story. Tears flow freely from Jamie's and my eyes.

Lord, she's been through so much!

Jamie and I both share how proud we are of our daughter.

Lord, thanks to You, I didn't miss out!

Months later, Jamie and I get away for the weekend to celebrate our birthdays. John approaches us when we return Sunday afternoon, "I've got to tell you about Shannon."

"Shannon? Is she okay? What happened?"

"It's bad, really bad."

"Okay, go ahead and tell us."

"One of her friends called her and said he was sick, so Shannon took some soup over to him."

"Uhm"

"When she got there, he wasn't sick, but asked her in. She went inside and he wanted to do more than she was willing. He did it anyway! She's a mess not only emotionally, but also physically."

"Did she contact the police, go to the hospital?"

"Yes, a friend took her both places."

The darkest grief washes over me.

Lord, You know what a godly woman she is! Why didn't You protect her?

Sleep evades me for weeks. Thoughts of how I can kill this man are a constant companion. Jamie and I talk, pray, and weep often over the disaster.

Lord, I don't know how to handle this. Maybe I'll go to a counselor.

The professional's voice is reassuring during our phone conversation. The following week, I go to see her. The office is a long rectangle; her desk is close to the door, ten to twelve feet away sit two wingback chairs. She sits at the desk.

It feels like she wants to be as far away from me and my problems as possible!

We visit for less than an hour while I cry and share about my daughter.

She gives me her "nugget" of help as our hour wraps up. "I want you to go home and think about what you're thinking about. I'll see you next…you said Wednesday will work, right?"

If I think about what I'm thinking about I'll kill this man! Nope, don't plan to come back.

Mechanically, I start my car.

Lord, I need help! Tell me what to do!

God nudges me as I drive home. "Stop at that Christian bookstore."

I pull into their parking lot; I enter the establishment.

This is dumb. Don't even know what I'm looking for!

"Walk down the aisle a little farther. Turn right and keep going. On the bottom shelf is your book. Yes, that's the one."

Hopelessly numb, I pay for the book and drive home.

Once in my living room, I grasp the book and pull it out of the plastic bag.

"Battlefield of the Mind" by Joyce Meyer?

"Look at the chapter titles."

Chapter seven's title is "Think About What You're Thinking About!"

That afternoon I dive into the material! Through Mrs. Meyer, God addresses worry, doubt, confusion, depression, anger, and feelings of condemnation by teaching how to deal with thoughts and think the way He thinks.

Little by little, my mind is conformed to Christ's teachings. I learn the importance of "taking every thought captive" as the Apostle Paul instructed in the book of 2 Corinthians. Several months later, I lead a class using Mrs. Meyer's book!

The Maestro helps the musician rub oil into my frame.

SYMPHONY MOVEMENT NO. 3

19

Empty Nest?

The following year Shannon starts mentioning how incredible one Narcotics Anonymous member is. One afternoon, she announces to me, "I want to have Shane over. He needs to talk with you and Dad."

"Okay, what about?"

"Well…things are pretty serious between us and we need to talk to both of you."

Dear Lord, no!

"Okay, how about Friday night?"

"I'll ask Shane!"

That evening, after Jamie and I go to bed, I proclaim the dreaded new, "Hon, Shannon's friend, Shane, is coming over Friday night. He wants to talk to us. Shannon says that things are getting serious."

"I told her not to date anyone from that program!"

"I know, but what can we do? She's twenty-two years old. If she thinks she's in love, we better meet him."

"Guess you're right. If she is in love, we have no choice. There's little we can do to stop her from marrying him."

Shannon excitedly gets ready early Friday evening. We soon hear a motorcycle roar up our driveway. She bounds down the stairs squealing, "He's here!"

With heavy hearts, Jamie and I plod to the entryway. When Shannon opens the front door, we get our first glimpse of her "heart-throb." Tattoos cover his neck and arms. A blond Mohawk salutes us. The Fu Manchu mustache and goatee complete the picture.

Jamie steps forward, extending his hand. I cringe. "I'm Jamie Royal, Shannon's Dad. Come on upstairs."

I wish you were wearing your police uniform, complete with holster, gun, and cuffs!

Shane shakes Jamie's hand.

I'm surprised he didn't give Jamie a high-five or fist bump!

Shannon leads Shane up the staircase. Shane proudly swaggers as only someone from the hood would.

Jamie and I sit in our favorite chairs. Shannon and Shane sit close to each other on the couch. Jamie breaks the silence. "Shannon said you want to talk to us."

"Yeah." He slides closer to our daughter.

Really? As though you're not close enough!

He puts his arm possessively around her. I try to hide my seething heart.

"Shannon and I are in love. She said I need to ask you this."

"Okay." Jamie folds his arms across his chest.

"Well, uh…um… I want permission to marry Shannon."

"Tell us about yourself."

"I grew up a little in California, and then my parents and I moved to Colorado Springs. You probably know I met Shannon at NA."

"Uh-huh. When did you start doing drugs?"

"I da know. Guess I was about thirteen. Got involved in a gang."

"How old are you?"

"I'm thirty-two."

"Ten years older than Shannon?"

"Yeah," smiling, he proudly pulls Shannon even closer.

"How did you start going to Narcotics Anonymous?"

Clearing his throat, Shane flippantly states, "The judge said I could either go to the Salvation Army or jail."

Everything a home-schooling mom and police officer dad want to hear.

"Why were you arrested?"

He answers with a shrug. "I had drugs in my pocket."

Jamie takes a deep breath, "Okay, continue."

"I went to the Salvation Army. It was the best thing I ever did! They read the Bible every day! They had classes about what we read. After several weeks, I asked Jesus into my life!" Shane's countenance brightens with each word.

Shannon interrupts, "Shane asked me out a year ago, but I said, 'No.' I liked what I saw at NA, but I waited a year to see if he was real or just doing a con. He shares at every meeting and now sometimes leads."

Jamie regains the conversation's reins, "Tell me more, Shane."

"Well, God became real while I was at the Salvation Army. I read the Bible every day. I started learning more."

The more he talks, the more my shoulders relax.

I actually like this guy. I understand a little of what Shannon sees in him.

By the end of the evening, Jamie and I give permission for them to get married.

Shannon informs us, "We plan to get married in six months."

Jamie acknowledges, "That's a good idea, I don't believe it's healthy to have too long of an engagement."

We all hug as they leave our house. Our phone rings within an hour. Jamie answers, "Hello. Uh-hm… I see…all right then… May 11. Love you, bye."

"What was that about?"

"Well, it seems they misunderstood our comments about a long engagement. They've set their wedding date for May 11."

"May 11! What're they thinking? That's only a little over a month away! Dad and Mom's fiftieth wedding anniversary is the eighteenth, just a week later! We've already mailed invitations to over one hundred people! Give me the phone! I've got to call Shannon back!"

Jamie gladly hands the phone to me. "Shannon, May 11 will not work! Mom and Dad's anniversary party is the next week! I won't be able to help with your wedding! That's only six weeks from now!"

"It won't be a problem, Mom. We're having a small wedding. I'll take care of everything."

"Who are you inviting to this small wedding?"

"Oh, you know, just our family, Shane's, some church friends, some of Dad's work buddies."

Lord, help me! You know I can't juggle too many things at once!

The following afternoon, Shannon comes upstairs beaming ear to ear. "Mom, you're not going to believe this! I called Holly's mom and she's now a wedding planner! She volunteered to plan my entire wedding!"

Thank You, Lord! Tension eases from my shoulders.

The weeks pass quickly. Shannon and I finally get a day together to find her wedding dress. She voices her wishes, "I don't want a regular wedding gown, just a simple white dress."

"Do you want to go by a bridal store? That way we can see what they have to offer."

"Nope, let's just run by Macy's and see what they have."

"All right."

Once inside, Shannon grabs three dresses off the racks. She tries two on and then states, "This is the one. Let's go."

I shouldn't be surprised. She's always hated shopping, but this is her wedding dress! So much for a mother/daughter day! There's no need to fuss, it's just my only daughter's wedding!

She chooses a friend from NA to sing. The only complication is that she's in a halfway house. Since she can't get out for practice, Shannon buys an accompaniment CD. Thankfully, she rehearses while incarcerated.

At the wedding rehearsal, one of Shane's sisters hugs me, "You're an answer to my prayers!"

"Thank you," I return the hug.

Wish I could say the same. Knowing you pray for your brother threads a tiny stitch of hope into my soul. Maybe Shannon is the answer to their prayers.

Shannon joins Jamie and me in the kitchen midmorning on her wedding day. "I'm getting ready to leave. One of Shane's sisters is a beautician. She's going to cut my hair. I'll see you at the church!"

"You're leaving? You're having someone cut your hair for the first time on your wedding day?"

"Yes, and yes. Bye!"

So much for our last morning together!

The wedding's an interesting cross-section of society. Throughout the sanctuary are family and church members, interspersed are plain-clothes police officers. The two rows against the back wall are people I don't know but look like they're from the Narcotics Anonymous group.

Who knows? Maybe a few Shane met in jail!

I can't help but shake my head at the irony of it all. When Shannon's friend sings, all those in the back grab their lighters, ignite them, and sway their torches to the music.

All told, over one hundred people were to attend the "small" wedding.

By ten thirty, Jamie and I are home. After a six-week engagement, our baby is married. My husband and I stand in our house's entryway. Exhausted physically and emotionally, we cling to each other. I sob on Jamie's shoulder. Too overwhelmed to talk, we go straight to bed.

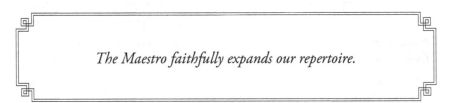

The Maestro faithfully expands our repertoire.

20

Doing daily tasks becomes more challenging for me, as each passing year as the multiple sclerosis progresses. One afternoon, I get groceries, drive home, park in the driveway, and exit the car. When I stand up, my left leg doesn't support me so I immediately collapse! Function returns after only a few seconds. That night I mention, "Jamie, the weirdest thing happened today…"

The concern on his face warms my heart. "We knew this day might come. We're going to need to eventually buy a one-story home. Why don't we go ahead and put our house on the market?"

"Think you're right. Let's do it!"

Our realtor, who specializes in finding homes for handicapped people, narrows our search to meet my needs. We find a home only a couple of weeks after our current one gets a contract!

We quickly move. The new one has a park only two blocks away! Jamie and I take advantage of the flat neighborhood by going for "strolls" every evening. (My walking's S… L… O… W!)

As empty nesters, we follow our routine of going to church every Sunday morning and evening. The night services hold an intimate closeness among the family of Christ. One evening, a good friend and I chat, "You haven't seen our new house! Why don't you and your hubby come for dinner? We can stop at a fast-food restaurant and bring the food to our place!"

"That sounds great!" We discuss options for take-out but can't agree.

"Why don't you get what you want, and we'll get what we want and then meet us at our house!"

"Perfect! It'll be so good to catch up! I've just got to run in the church office and grab something. I'll be right back!"

She's back within a few minutes. "I ran into Karen and told her what we're doing. She's so excited she and Don want to join us! Then, Donna overheard, so they're coming too!"

"Great! Let's grab our guys and we'll see you when you get to our new home!"

I explain the plans to Jamie as he buckles his seatbelt. "You did what? How many people? They're all bringing dinner?"

"Things just snowballed, honey. No, they're each bringing their own dinner." He shakes his head.

The impromptu party's filled with lots of laughter and good-natured ribbing. Our music pastor asks, "Denise, I know we're supposed to bring our own food, but will it break the rules if you let me use some of your catsup?" The group roars!

One week I feel led to tell our class about the miracle God did in our marriage. As I share, tears flow uncontrollably.

Lord, I don't know why I'm crying. You put our marriage back together. Jamie and I are so in love, it's hard to believe we ever had serious problems and almost divorced!

His tender words pierce my heart. "You accepted Jamie's apology, but you don't believe I forgave you for turning away from Me. You need to accept my forgiveness for you!"

Torrents of tears cascade down my cheeks as I embrace His love. *You're right, Lord! I do accept Your love and forgiveness! Thank You!*

Both our kids are shocked that we bought a house larger than our last one. Their words are almost identical, "I thought you were going to downsize!"

*****

Jamie and I love our time alone. We play cards, dice games, or Parcheesi regularly. If I'm too sick to sit at our table, Jamie pulls a TV tray up to the couch so we can play in the den. Our television's rarely on. He frequently comments, "If I die tonight, I'd die a happy man! I've had a full, great life!" I agree.

We join a church closer to our new home where God's activity is obvious in members' lives and testimonies. Jamie and I gain several new friends.

The two of us occasionally discuss the unfinished basement. He mentions, "You know, if we finished a bathroom and bedroom down there, if something happens to one of our dads, one of our moms could move down there."

"Yeah, we could even include a living room and small kitchenette. If we need to, we can put in a chairlift for the stairs!"

Jamie starts the construction the next spring. When John hears we have a spare bedroom, he finagles his dad into letting him be our basement "tenant." He only sleeps at our house. His life is full with work, his church, and friends.

We tease each other saying, "We should've known better! There's a saying, 'If you build it they will come.'"

Our life's good, but we're not perfect! One night, after almost twenty-nine years of marriage, we have a disagreement.

Okay, an argument. Jamie's so obstinate!

We're discussing something, and then he turns his back on me, walks out our sliding glass door, and closes it! There he sits at our patio table with his back to me! Right in the middle of our disagreement!

I can't believe his nerve!

I calmly walk to the patio door, lock it, and then I go into our bedroom and get ready for bed.

He can just walk around the house and let himself in.

Within a few minutes I hear knocking on the glass door.

Hmph. Go around and let your own dumb self in!

Soon he's pounding on the bathroom window, shouting, "Let me in!"

"Let yourself in!"

"The gate's locked!"

Oh, didn't think of that. Oh well, he's jumped plenty of fences.

"Jump the fence!"
"We cemented up to the opposite side of the fence!"
Oops! I'm not that angry!
"Okay." I relent and repent. I sheepishly unlock the door.

*****

In 2009, Christians everywhere are talking about the "prayer of Jabez."[7] Our Bible study groups delve into the book by Bruce Wilkinson about this man's prayer, "Lord, expand our territory!"

Jamie leads the two of us in earnest prayer, "God, please expand our realm of influence, allow us to reach more people than we think possible!"

As the 2010 holidays approach, I eagerly decorate our home.

I'm so glad Shannon moved back to the Springs! Everyone will be here for the holiday!

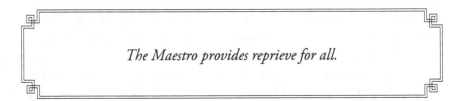

The Maestro provides reprieve for all.

21

Christmas 2010 is to be unforgettable for my family and me. None of us have any idea what God has in store. I remember it now as a season of miracles.

On December eleventh, Jamie and I meet his college buddy, Michael, and his wife, Irene, for a meal. Michael is home for Christmas from his foreign duty assignment. After being friends since their college days, Michael seems like Jamie's brother. Over thirty years ago, he was the best man at our wedding. The guys enjoy fishing, camping, and sharing stories. Irene and I are quiet, studious, indoor gals.

Thank You, Lord, for lifetime friends!

The following morning, Jamie continues his normal routine of making Sunday breakfast. He makes Pillsbury turnovers. It's December 12, 2021. *Thank You, Lord, for this guy!*

We go to our church's worship service then our class. Afterward, we ask a visiting couple to come to our house for lunch. That evening, we attend our church's evening Christmas program. While driving home, our traffic lane has a green left turn arrow. Jamie turns deeply toward stopped vehicles facing us.

He's not turning! "Turn! Turn!" I yell. He seems to "wake up" from some kind of trance.

Thank You, Lord, that the traffic was stopped for the light!
Jamie must be super tired. He's usually a great driver!

On December 13, Jamie wakes up at his normal time, eats breakfast, and then heads to work.

We learned many years ago that days go better if I sleep longer. Shortly after I get out of bed, our phone rings.

"Hello?"

It's Jamie. "Honey, would you set up an appointment with our general practice doctor? I'm taking a sick day."

"Sure, what's going on?"

"Something strange is happening. While driving to work, I accidentally drove onto the center median, and then I instantly corrected my path. When I got to the sub-station's employee parking lot, I drove past the entrance, backed up, and then entered. When I got inside, I started up my computer and could hardly read the screen. I talked to the sergeant and asked him if I could take a sick day. It's like my vision's weird. Don't know why. Some of the guys here said maybe I have a type of migraine. My boss will drive me home."

When Jamie gets home, I inform him, "Our doctor's booked. They can get you in tomorrow. What do you want to do?"

"Why don't we just go down to the urgent care that shares our GP's office?"

After arriving, Jamie checks in and sits beside me. One of our general practice doctor's receptionists asks, "Excuse me. Did you call earlier for an appointment?"

Jamie answers, "Yeah, but you said his schedule is full."

"That's right, but one of his associates has an opening in five minutes. Would you like to see him?"

Jamie nods, gives the thumbs up sign, and states, "Sure! Thanks!"

Thank you, Lord, for opening doors so we don't have to wait! Within minutes, the nurse escorts us into the doctor's examination room. He enters, "What's going on?"

"Well, sir, I seem to be having some kind of vision problem, or maybe it's a migraine. I can't see too much on my left side."

"Okay. Let me take a look. Mm-Hm. Mm-Hm. Okay, let me look in your other eye. Okay, okay. Are you having a headache?"

"Yeah, I guess a minor one."

"Okay, Mr. Royal. I want you to go home and rest. Mrs. Royal?" I nod. "I want you to call and get Jamie into a neurologist office for an exam."

"Okay?" *Why a neurologist? That's weird.*

"Here's a list of doctors I recommend. That'll be all."

Lord, I've got personal experience with neurologists. It usually takes five to six months to get an appointment. Help get us into one sooner!

Once home, Jamie informs me, "I think I'll take a nap."

I pick up the phone and ask our friends for their prayers. Then, I dial the first two numbers trying to get an appointment. Those two tell me exactly what I expect, "It'll be a five- to six-month wait."

Before calling the third, I pray. *Lord, help us. Show me what to do.* "Try a different tactic."

"You've reached Dr. Smith's office. How can I help you?"

"My husband needs to see a neurologist as soon as possible."

"Yes, ma'am. Let me check our appointment book. Okay, we can see your husband on May…"

"Ma'am," I interrupted, "my husband is a police officer and can't go back to work until he's seen by a neurologist. Would you please call if you have any cancellations?"

"Yes, I certainly will. What is your phone number and your husband's name?"

Okay, Lord. We need a miracle. We're counting on You!

I call friends. "Please pray that an appointment will open up soon."

Jamie and I rest the remainder of the day.

Our phone rings first thing on December 14. "Is this Mrs. Royal?"

"Yes."

"You called our office about an appointment for your husband?"

"Yes."

"Well, someone just called to say they can't make their appointment. Could you be here within the hour?"

"Yes! We'll be there!"

Thank you, Lord, for opening an appointment for us!

I call our prayer partners.

Within moments of arriving, the nurse ushers us into an examination room. The doctor soon enters. Without looking up from the chart in his hands, he sits down. "Okay, what brings you in today?"

Jamie answers, "I seem to be having some kind of vision problem."

"And how long has this been going on?"

"Since Sunday evening."

"What?" The doctor's mouth falls open; his clipboard drops to his lap. He shouts, "How on earth did you get into my office? I have people waiting five months to see me!"

Mumbling as he leaves the room, "I'll speak to my staff about this!"

I know Who arranged this appointment. Thank You, Thank You, Thank You, Lord!

Before we leave the office, the receptionist hands Jamie orders to have an MRI.

Lord, I know from my own experience the normal progression of these tests: a week or two before the test is done. Lord, please help Jamie get the MRI as soon as possible!

We go home where I first call prayer partners, and then the hospital.

"Hmm, it seems we have an opening tomorrow morning. Can you be here at…"

"Yes!"

Thank You Lord, for another miracle!

On the morning of December 15, I drive Jamie to the hospital and sit in the waiting room as he has the MRI. As we leave the office, the technician walks Jamie to the exit door. Because of Jamie's pleasant, friendly manner and charismatic personality, conversations often continue long after scheduled interactions. This seems to be one of those instances. The technician shakes hands with Jamie as they walk.

Thank You for having things go so quickly!

After we climb into our vehicle, Jamie shares, "That was kind of weird!"

"What?"

"When we left, the technician squeezed my hand extra firm. He looked like he was about to cry."

Since Jamie's scheduled to change sub-stations today, we swing by his last precinct to grab his things to move to the next location. Then we stop to grab a quick lunch before I take Jamie to his new office.

As he closes the car door, smiling, he comments, "See you later! Hope you have a good afternoon! Love you!"

"Love you too!" I return a smile.

My heart still melts at his whimsical grin! I'm ready for a nap! It'll be good to get home.

Thank You, Lord, for being so good.

Our landline phone's ringing as I enter the house. Breathlessly, I grab the receiver. "Yes?"

Jamie softly states, "Honey, it's me."

"What's up?"

Silence hangs in the air.

"Baby, the doctor's office has been trying to call me. I forgot my cell phone at home today. As soon as I went inside the sub-station, one of the ladies told me I needed to call the neurologist."

"Okay?"

"Baby, they believe I have a brain tumor. I'm supposed to get to the hospital as soon as possible. Gary says he'll come and get you and drive us to the hospital."

I feel as though I've been kicked in the stomach. "Okay. I'll be ready."

Ready? Ready for what? Lord, give me Your strength. Give me Your grace!

Trembling fingers dial prayer warriors after I throw a few items in an overnight bag.

Jamie's admitted and placed in a typical hospital room. The doctor told him surgery will be scheduled sooner if Jamie's admitted. The operation's scheduled for Saturday morning, three days later.

Jamie feels normal. After an evening of constant laughter and visitors, the hospital staff moves us to a room with a large guest room next door. Jamie, dressed in comfy sweatpants, enjoys his barrage of visitors.

I hang out at the hospital all day on December 16. Jamie has more visitors than I can remember. The day is filled with more stories and laughter.

The next day, one of Jamie's friends prays in his hospital room and accepts Jesus as his Lord and Savior.

Thank You, Lord, for bringing good out of all this craziness!

As surgery looms nearer, both Jamie and I grow anxious. We pray together and just hold each other. Jamie repeats last requests and his "living will."

"Denise, I don't know if I'll live through the surgery, or if my mind will be okay. But I want you to know I love you. You've been a great wife. I'm sorry for what I put you through."

"This isn't your fault."

"I don't mean this. I mean…"

"Oh, that."

"Yeah, that."

"You know God healed my heart, and I forgave you years ago. Have I ever brought it up?"

"No."

"Then there's no need to bring it up now. I love you. I love you now and no matter what happens tomorrow."

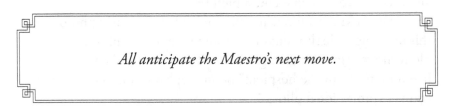

All anticipate the Maestro's next move.

22

We gather in the large "guest overflow" room on December 18. Jamie keeps us all entertained and laughing, reciting several of his favorite "war" stories.

As the moments tick by, all grow solemn. Jamie's and my parents, our kids, Jamie's little brother and sister-in-law, Ronnie and Ann, Michael, Irene and Niki, and Gary all wait with us for the nurse to take him to the operating room. The mood early this morning remains light. Hours pass.

Shannon approaches me and whispers in my ear, "I'd like a family picture."

"Really?"

Thank You, Lord. You know because Shannon's been so sick, she hasn't let us take her picture in years.

I glance around the room. *Mostly cops. Great! I don't want a crime scene photo!*

My gaze stops on Gary. *His daughter and son-in-law are photographers!*

I quickly make my way to his side. "Gary, do you think Stephanie and Stephen could come take a picture?"

"I don't know. I'll call and find out! They were on a photo shoot this morning!" He slips out of the room with his cell phone to his ear. He reenters grinning, giving a nod. "They just finished up and are five minutes from the hospital!" Soon Stephanie and Stephen arrive and take professional photos!

Thank You, Lord, for changing Shannon's heart! Thank You for Stephanie and Stephen!

As the minutes draw nearer to surgery, all grow even quieter and more contemplative. Shannon gets up and sits on her daddy's lap, massaging his neck.

Jamie asks, "Denise, would you hand me my Bible?" I give it to him. "I'd like to read something that I've been reading a lot." Jamie turns in his Bible, "Here it is, Psalm 23 (NIV), 'The Lord is my shepherd, I shall not be in want. He makes me lie down in green pastures, he leads me beside quiet waters, he restores my soul. He guides me in paths of righteousness for his name's sake. Even though I walk through the valley of the shadow of death, I will fear no evil, for you are with me; your rod and your staff, they comfort me. You prepare a table before me in the presence of my enemies. You anoint my head with oil. My cup overflows. Surely goodness and love will follow me all the days of my life, and I will dwell in the house of the Lord forever.' I'd like Pat to lead us in prayer."

We all join hands; Dad prays.

Jamie speaks, "I want each of you to know how much I love you. There's no guarantee for any of us, but there's no guarantee that I will wake up from this surgery. No matter what happens, remember I love you." His gaze passes around the room, slowing locking eyes with each person.

A man arrives, "Are you Jamie Royal?"

"Yes, sir. That'd be me."

"I'm here to take you to preop. Can you get into the wheelchair or do you need help?"

Jamie stands and then walks over, and sits in the chair. "Here we go. Love you all!"

I tell the group, "See you all in the waiting room."

Within minutes, Jamie, the kids, and I are in the preop room. Fabric curtains separate us from other patients. After data is checked and rechecked, the nurse excuses himself. "The surgeon and anesthesiologist will be in soon."

Our little family stands close to his bedside; Jamie starts telling silly stories. One leads to another. Shannon and I are in tears from laughter when the surgeon steps through the curtains. "Mr. Royal?" he extends his hand.

Jamie gives him a firm handshake, "Yes, sir."

"We're ready for you. We will take you first, for an up-to-the-minute MRI. Then I'm going to place what we call "life-savers" on your scalp. They will show me precisely where I need to work. Do you have any questions?"

"No, sir."

"Would it be all right if I pray with you?"

"Please! I appreciate it!"

The surgeon takes Jamie's hand and bows his head. "Dear God, I ask You to guide me as I perform this surgery. Be with everyone in the operating room. Thank You for Mr. Royal and his family. I ask You to be with each of them. Amen. Mrs. Royal… I'll see you after the surgery in the waiting room." *Thank You, Lord, for a surgeon whose faith is in You!*

A nurse takes the man I love, the man with whom I've spent my life, to surgery.

The enemy relentlessly slings questions into my mind. *Will he wake up from this surgery? Will he be the same mentally? Will he be able to talk? Walk? Feed himself?*

Lord, be with Jamie. Be with the surgeon. Be with the kids and me! We need your peace!

Throughout the day Shannon informs me, "I can't reach Shane. He knows Dad's having surgery! Where is he?"

Because my mind is only focuses on Jamie's surgery, I reply, "Don't know, honey. He'll likely call later."

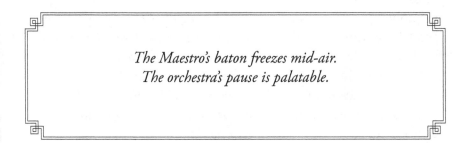

The Maestro's baton freezes mid-air.
The orchestra's pause is palatable.

23

Family members bring lunch so we eat during Jamie's surgery. *Thank You, Lord, for loving family and coworkers taking care of our needs.*

Our longtime friend, Alta, a lab worker, volunteers to work today so she can do the tests on Jamie's tumor. A few hours after we finish lunch, she comes into the waiting room. I see her standing by the door. I get up and walk over to her. She hugs me tightly. "It's not good," she whispers. "It's the worst of the worst. Don't let the doctor know I told you." Her arms squeeze firmer before she turns and leaves. *Thank You, Lord, for Alta delivering this news.*

I walk back to my family. "That was my friend. She did the lab work. She said it's not good, the worst of the worst. We can't let the doctor know that she told us anything. He will be in soon."

Jim and Dad both lead us in prayer.

Dr. McVickers approaches our group. "He's out of surgery. He should be moved to intensive care within an hour. The surgery went well. We won't have final biopsy results until Monday. The tumor looked bad. I believe it was a glioblastoma. If that's the case, he'll live another three to five years at most."

"Sir, please don't tell him tonight."

"Ma'am, I usually inform the patient as soon as I see them."

"But I know my husband. Please don't tell him tonight. Let him get one night of rest before he hears the news."

"I can't make any promises."

Within an hour, Jamie's wheeled into intensive care. He smiles, still groggy.

I report as I give his cheek a peck, "Hey, babe! You look great!"
One by one, friends and family disperse.

A nurse comments, "You may as well go home and get some rest. He'll be getting the best of care while in ICU." Much later, one of my kids drives me home.

The following morning, I trip while making my way to the bathroom. My rib hits my sewing machine cabinet on the way down.

"Ow!" *Lord, help! I can't believe I'm so clumsy!*

I get ready for my parents to drive me to the hospital. "Dad, Mom, I hate this, but would you please take me by the after-hours clinic? I fell this morning and think I broke my rib."

"Oh, Denise! Are you okay?"

"Yeah, just clumsy. I think I need some pain medicine though."

We make the detour to the clinic before going to the hospital. Sure enough, I fractured a rib. *Is this really necessary, Lord?*

"Trust Me."

Okay, if You say so.

Jamie's sitting up eating breakfast as we arrive. "Good morning!"

"Good morning to you! You don't look like you just had brain surgery!"

"They're moving me to another room as soon as one opens up!"

"Great! I'll get your things packed up."

"Um, Denise?"

"Yeah."

"The surgeon came by this morning. He said the tumor was cancerous. He said I have three to five years."

I walk to his side and sit on the bedside. Grasping Jamie's hand my eyes tear up. "I'm sorry, honey. We'll go through this together. I love you." I put my head against his chest.

After he finishes breakfast, Jamie and I are sent to occupational rehabilitation therapy. I watch my strong, healthy husband struggle to walk up and down three stairs. Intense concentration's evident as he reads aloud a few sentences. Writing is as much of a challenge.

The therapist directs, "When you get home, help your husband work on the things I've listed on this paper."

"Yes, ma'am."

We're taken from there to Jamie's new room. Exhausted, Jamie sleeps a couple of hours.

The next morning, the first neurologist we'd seen pops in and apologizes for his previous reaction. He was the one who was angry at his staff for scheduling Jamie's office visit. *That's kind of him.* Jamie and the doc shake hands.

Tuesday an oncologist comes into Jamie's hospital room and introduces himself. "We've got the pathology report back. It's the worst kind of brain cancer. If you do chemotherapy, radiation, and have more brain surgeries, you might live a year."

Jamie gulps and takes a deep breath. He glances at me before asking, "And what if I do nothing?"

"Three to four months."

"Okay, I choose option B. I know where I'm going when I die."

"All right, sir. Here's my card. If you want to discuss it after you've had time to reconsider, give my office a call."

"Thank you, sir, but there will be no reconsidering."

The following morning, Jamie speaks as I enter his room. "Denise, I'm afraid the surgery really messed my brain up. I wake up and think the bathroom is on the right, but it's on the left. Then the next time I wake up, I think the john's on the left, but it's on the right."

Smiling, I sit on his bedside and hold his hand. "Honey, it's not your brain, the staff is messing with your mind. You've been in the hospital five days and they've moved you four times!"

We enjoy stress-relieving laughter.

The hospital releases us within a few hours.

A hospice nurse comes by our house later.

I notify friends of Jamie's diagnosis and prognosis. Some fly in for a few hours Christmas Day. We go to my parents' house for lunch and a gift exchange.

The same question seems to be on everyone's mind...what do you give someone who only has a few months to live?

Eight days after Jamie's surgery, our pastor allows Jamie to share what God has been doing in his life at our church service. A church member films the testimony.

Several other churches request Jamie to speak at their churches. Jamie calls these talks "Fearless Ministry."

John approaches us late that afternoon. Mom and Dad, I need to fill you in about Shannon and Shane."

"Oh, yeah! He flew in yesterday to spend Christmas with Shannon! How is he?"

"Well… Shannon drove to DIA to get him and he drove them to our house."

"Are they here?"

"Mom, wait, Shane told Shannon he wants a divorce."

Jamie erupts, "What? What kind of man…"

John continues, "Shannon was so upset, I drove her to Uncle Ronnie's. I didn't want to wake you. It's only been a few days since your surgery."

We don't see Shannon for several hours.

Jamie's unable to sleep the first two weeks after his surgery. Every night of the first week when I roll over in bed, he's not there. I climb out of bed, grab my robe and start searching for him. "Jamie, where are you? Honey?"

He shouts back, "I'm in the office. Sorry, couldn't sleep so decided to go through some of our files" or "I'm in the den, studying my Bible, getting ready for next week."

"It's the middle of the night, please come back to bed!"

"There's no use in lying down. I can't sleep. Go back to bed, I'm fine. Love you!"

One night he doesn't answer. I search the upstairs. "Jamie! Where are you?" I even look in the garage. *No, he didn't drive anywhere. What if he went for a walk and got disoriented?*

"Honey! Jamie!" No answer. Our son's gone for the night.

I do not want to go down to the basement! What if he's collapsed down there? What if he died down there? No, I can't go down there! My heart's pounding!

I kneel and pray, "God, I need your help! Show me what to do! I sit in the living room for what seems an eternity. Finally, I reluctantly call our neighbor, one of Jamie's coworkers. "John? It's Denise. Sorry to wake you!"

His voice grumbles as he clears his throat. "It's okay. What's up?"

"Well, I can't find Jamie. He's not upstairs and is not answering when I yell down the stairs. I'm afraid to go down there. What if something's happened to him down there?"

"I'll be right over."

"Thanks."

I open my front door a few minutes later. "Thanks for coming over."

"It's not a problem. I'll go check your basement."

I stand at the top of the stairs. "No, he's not down there. Why don't we sit and give this some thought?"

"Yeah. What if he went for a walk and got disoriented?"

"Has he been confused since the surgery?"

"Not really, but I don't know what to expect after brain surgery. Should we put out an APB so officers will be looking for him?"

"No, I'll just drive around the neighborhood and see if I spot him. I'll be back in a few."

I lock the door behind him. Kneeling, I plead with my Lord. *God, please show John where Jamie is! Help us, Lord! Be with Jamie! Help him be safe!* I get off my knees and sit on our love seat. Minutes drag till our neighbor returns.

"I didn't find him. I guess I will call the sub-station and ask the patrol officers to start looking for him."

I hand him my phone. "Hi, this is Ford. I need patrol to start looking for Jam...what's that? He's there? Okay, thanks! Talk to you in the morning."

My voice returns, "Jamie's at the sub-station? How'd he get there?"

Our neighbor shakes his head. Grinning, he explains, "Jamie couldn't sleep so he called the sub-station and asked an officer to come by and get him. He's been down there the whole-time telling stories!"

My shoulders relax. "Thank you. Sorry to bother you!"

"Not a problem. Jamie would do the same for me if I needed him. Night."

"Night."

I don't believe this man! We'll have a talk...in the morning!

The next day I buy a magnetic whiteboard with an attached marker. "If you leave, write down where you've gone! We're not going to have a repeat of yesterday!" Jamie, grinning, shrugs sheepishly.

The second week, he's still not sleeping. I decide Jamie will be fine. I don't need to babysit him. I've got to get some sleep so I don't get sick! I'll see him in the morning.

Our family starts living a new "normal." Jamie speaks at a different church every Sunday and often on Saturdays. Most hours he's home our house is packed with police department employees. Our front door needs to be a revolving one. We average fifty to seventy visitors a day.

A close friend, Janet Sandeen, volunteers to cook meals for our family. "Janet, I appreciate your offer but my family is now on three different diets! My MS diet, Shannon's limited diet, and now Jamie's on an anti-cancer diet! I can't ask you to do that!"

"You didn't ask. I'm volunteering! Will four o'clock be okay for me to bring dinner by?"

"Sure. Thank you! I can't believe you're doing this!"

"When people offer to bring meals just suggest they donate money to me to cover the cost of the food."

"Definitely, thanks!" *Thank You, Lord, for Your family!*

*****

Knowing his parents need to spend as much time as possible with their son, Shannon drives Jamie to his parents' home every Monday and brings him home the following Wednesday.

His folks need to see their boy as much as possible in the time he has left.

While he's gone, I rest and grieve. My friend, Kathy, is unemployed and tells me, "Call me any time. I want to be here for you."

My sorrow's very dark most of the nights Jamie's gone, so I take Kathy up on the offer. I even call in the middle of the night.

Lord, thank You for a single friend and even for her unemployment right now!

She cries, listens, and prays with me. My energy renews so I'm able to greet the throngs of Jamie's guests throughout the next few days.

When we're outside our home, Jamie now needs a steadying arm to keep from walking into things. He talks to everyone within earshot whenever he's out, "Hi, I've got brain cancer and although I've only got a few months to live, I have complete peace. Be sure you know where you're going when you die. Be sure you know Jesus, be sure you tell your family and friends that you love them as often as you can!"

He and I delve into deep discussions. "Denise, after I'm gone, I want you to know that you've been a great wife! I apologize again for my unfaithfulness. You're a young woman, feel free to remarry."

Through tears, I reply, "You're a wonderful husband! You don't need to apologize. The affair is in the past. God forgave. I'm glad God enabled us to stay together! I enjoy every moment we're together!"

Embracing me, he continues, "And, Denise, finish the book. People need to hear about God's goodness!"

*****

Ron, Buck, and Gary come as often as they're able. Honestly, Ron practically lives at our house. They relive "war stories" from work and talk of fishing this summer.

It's hard to believe it's only been seven weeks since Jamie's surgery! He continues to speak at churches on the weekends.

Saturday, February 12, 2011, brings sunshine. Jamie rises early for two speaking engagements. After speaking at a breakfast and again at a lunch, Jamie meets two friends he hasn't seen in years. He's determined to set things right in broken relationships.

Since Jamie's scheduled to speak for the tenth time in the morning at another church, we go to bed early. The next morning, I shut the alarm off as soon as it rings and rub Jamie's back. "Honey, it's time to get up."

"I'm not feeling well. I was awake most of the night with a headache."

"Sorry, babe. Do you want me to call the church or do you still want to speak?"

"I'm afraid I can't speak today. Would you mind calling the church?"

"Not at all," I crawl out of bed.

"I'm going to stay in bed and try to get more sleep."

"Okay."

After the phone call, I cook and eat breakfast, spend time with the Lord; read my Bible and pray. I put lunch in the crock pot, before deciding to check on Jamie.

"Hey, baby, are you feeling any better?"

"No. Would you mind coming back to bed? I can't seem to get warm."

I snuggle under the warm covers. Soon I hear Jamie's breathing relax as he drifts off to sleep. I awaken about an hour later.

Wow! I wasn't expecting to sleep!

I sense Jamie's also waking. "Can you help me?" he asks. "I can't seem to get out of bed."

"Sure." I hold Jamie's arms as he pulls himself up. As he walks into the bathroom, I walk behind, steadying him. Standing before the sink Jamie slowly loses his balance. His body tilts to the left. His head gently hits the wall.

Something's happened to him!

"Do you want to get back in bed or go to the den?"

"The den."

Gently, I guide him to the den and settle him into his recliner.

I walk into the kitchen and call hospice. "I think my husband may have had a stroke. Would you send a nurse out?"

Within two hours our nurse arrives. She completes a thorough exam. "No, it's not a stroke. It's the tumor. It's regrown and is causing the loss of use of his left side. This might just be a speed bump, or it might be the beginning of the end. We won't know for two days. Then it should be clear. I'll have a hospital bed brought over this afternoon. He's also lost use of his right arm, right leg, and most of his vision."

After letting her out, I breathe deeply. *Lord, I need Your strength! Thank You for Your peace I'm cocooned in. I know this isn't a speed bump. I know this is the beginning of the end.*

I pick up the phone and make the necessary family calls, giving each the update and ask anyone living outside of Colorado to come home.

Knowing it will take days for Michael to get home from the Middle East, I call Irene. "Irene? It's Denise."

"Hi, Denise. What's up?"

"Jamie took a turn for the worse. Would you call Michael? I think this is the end."

"I'm sorry! Do you need anything?"

"No. But Michael wanted to know when things were getting close."

"I'll call him right now."

Somberly, John, Shannon, and I clear the den furniture making room for the hospital bed. It's delivered a couple of hours later.

Jamie's older brother, Bob, arrives Monday morning, his little brother, Jeff, Tuesday. Jamie's closest friends Ron, Gary, and Buck take turns feeding him. Shannon cooks her dad's favorite foods.

Tuesday afternoon my mom hugs me. "Denise, why don't you lie down? Get some rest while you can."

Emotionally exhausted, I don't argue. "Okay." As I lay on my bed, tears flow freely. God gently whispers to me. "Denise, after Jamie dies you will experience grief. Allow yourself to cry. I understand grief. I made your tears. But after each time, get up and praise Me for the time you had together. That will make the enemy not want to make your grief last too long nor be as deep."

Immediately, refreshing strength comes over me. I climb out of bed and rejoin the others in the den.

By Wednesday morning, Jamie labors to breathe. His eyes are constantly closed. Although most of the police personnel haven't come since Jamie ended up in the hospital bed, our house is still packed with people. Many higher-ranking police officials come to show their support. We whisper our conversation never knowing if Jamie is awake or asleep. His pain medicine is increased to help with his headache. Occasionally, Jamie surprises us by joining in the conversation or retelling one of his stories.

Midmorning Wednesday, our doorbell rings. Michael enters the house and approaches Jamie. Without opening his eyes, Jamie exclaims, "Thanks for coming, Michael."

Michael quickly squeezes Jamie's hand. He softly says, "Made it as soon as I could!"

By Thursday, only close family and friends are present. All day Jamie labors to breathe. I'd heard of a "death rattle" but never personally heard it before. The sound seems to echo off our walls.

Jeff's wife, Sandy, softly sings, "Thank You for Giving to the Lord."[8] I ask my and Jamie's parents to tell him "goodbye." They each spend several moments alone with him. Then one by one we gather in the living room.

Around 10:00 p.m., Gary calls me aside. "Denise, I have my bagpipes in the car. Can I play the songs I plan on playing at the funeral so Jamie can hear them?" I nod.

Gary exits our home then stands outside playing "Amazing Grace." Wanting Jamie to hear, I open the front door and windows. As I gaze outside, I'm awestruck by the sight. The full moon back-lights Gary standing in the middle of our street. A little after midnight Gary and my parents leave.

The rest of us sit for over an hour in silence in our living room. Each of us is deep within our own thoughts and prayers. I subconsciously tuned out Jamie's death rattle hours ago. I'm surprised when John walks slowly out of the den. I didn't realize neither he nor Shannon are in the living room with the rest of us. John stands between the kitchen and living room.

My son softly speaks, "He's gone." Then he turns, picks up the phone and calls the police department. "Hello, this is John Royal. My dad is detective Jamie Royal. Would you please put out the call that there is an officer down? My dad just died. Thank you." I hear him hang up the phone and dial another number. *My brave son's calling hospice.*

I go into my bedroom where I throw myself across my bed, sobbing. Mom comes in and places her hand on my back. Between sobs I wail, "He took the wrong one!"

"No. God doesn't make mistakes, honey."

God, I know You don't make mistakes…but…taking me would make more sense. Jamie was the healthy one. No one would be surprised if it were me or Shannon!

Thirty years, six months, and sixteen days after our wedding, Jamie's gone. I am shrouded in grief.

As though someone turns off a power switch, the drum stops.
"How can the symphony continue without
the drum?" I question my Lord.
"How will we know when to join in or pause?"
"You'll watch and wait for Me."
I gulp and reply, "Okay, sir, but You're going
to have to help me relearn."
He gently answers, "I will."

SYMPHONY
MOVEMENT
NO. 4

24

The morning after Jamie dies, Shannon's asleep in our guest room while John and I sit in the empty den. The hospice bed's gone; furniture's back in place as though the past week hasn't occurred.

John softly interjects, "Last night after everyone but the Royal family left, I told Dad, 'Everyone's gone. It's okay for you to go now.' A few moments later Dad relaxed and breathed his last breath."

"John, I'm proud of you. Thank you for stepping in and becoming the man of our home."

The chief of police, a deputy chief, two sergeants, and our pastor meet with me this afternoon to plan the funeral. We all gather around our dining room table. Conversations erupt. My head swirls. "Excuse me, excuse me, because of the multiple sclerosis…" All eyes focus on me. "I can't handle more than one conversation going on at a time. Please limit talking."

The police chief took over, "Okay, Mrs. Royal, when should we do the flag presentation?"

I start to answer as three other conversations break out. "Excuse me!" My fist forcefully hits the solid oak. "Since you don't seem to understand, from now on if you want to speak, raise your hand! You can say something after I call on you!"

The meeting resumes following my rules. The chief of police raises his hand first. I blush. *Jamie would be shocked if he were here!* "Yes, sir?"

I know that since Jamie was in the motorcycle unit, they would love to escort you and your family to the funeral, if you'd like that."

"Sir, we would be honored. Thank you."

Preparations begin as other details are discussed.

My sister, Cindy, calls later, "Hi Denise. I'm so sorry! Wish I was there to give you a hug! I hate to tell you, but I can't come for the funeral. You know I just started my job and can't get more time off."

"Cindy, please don't worry about it. You and Jeff were just here last month."

"I love you and am praying for you. I hope you can come to see me in a month or two!"

"That'll be great! Thanks for your love! Bye."

Angel and Mark book flights immediately. Kathy drives down from Estes Park. Janet continues bringing food. Friends from all over the United States call and, most importantly, pray for us.

Angel and Mark stay at a hotel. Kathy comes into town two days before the funeral. She stays at one of her friend's house. Donna and Terry drive up from Albuquerque so they can attend the service.

The afternoon of the funeral, my family climbs into the police van when the motorcade arrives. Shannon and her cousin, and John and a friend go in separate vehicles. Tears pool in my eyes when a civilian exits his car and salutes.

I never understood how much that means!

Because so many people come to show their respect, the service starts at least 30 minutes later than planned.

An officer finally comes and announces, "We're ready for you."

The group stands as one mourning heap. Shannon, a deputy chief, and I end the procession. Shannon's too sick to walk most of the way so the deputy chief carries her. The folding of the flag and gun salute begin the service. Gary, Jamie's friend and sergeant, plays the bagpipe. Then my sister-in-law sings "If You Could See Me Now."[9] Michael, Gary, Ronnie, and Shannon share eulogies. Afterward, my pastor starts speaking. Within ten minutes, a lady from the building's staff gives an abrupt "time's up" signal, the service ends, and we're quickly ushered out.

Close friends and family come to the house afterward. We share stories; laughter and tears flow freely. *Lord, thank You for the sacrifices of my friends!*

Tonight, I cry. *Lord, why did the funeral end unfinished? The pastor didn't even get to give the plan of salvation!*

God whispers to my soul, "That's because I'm not finished with Fearless Ministry. I want you to have a DVD made of Jamie sharing his testimony. I want people to hear what I said through Jamie."

"Okay, but I don't know how to do that!"

"That's okay. I do and I will."

His peace remains, cocooning me.

A few days later, I walk toward our front door. Jamie's shoes are by the closet, right where he'd kicked them off. I collapse in tears. Shannon runs, sits beside me, and holds me. We sob together.

Before the weekend, I recall a friend's advice when she was widowed very young, "Go back to church as soon as possible!" On Sunday, I attend church.

Don't know why I'm running late. I should be able to get there on time! Guess putting the walker in the car slowed me down.

When I enter my Sunday morning classroom ten minutes late, the entire class stands, applauds, and then immediately swarm around to embrace me. *Thank You, Lord, for showing me love!*

The next week's a blur. Shannon's admitted to the hospital to treat the staph infection she's dealing with at home. She's released for a few days then readmitted for pancreatic problems.

My mind's numb. Mom comes to my house nearly every day. Janet continues bringing meals. John keeps working. Shannon works when not hospitalized. My life's consumed with paperwork and bills.

Can't wait till April 22! That's when I'm flying to my sister's for ten days!

Shannon stays with me the first week and then goes back to her house. She needs time to grieve over not only losing her dad but also her husband. Before leaving me alone, she buys an electric blanket. She places it only on Jamie's side of the bed and loans me her body pillow. Having warmth and the pillow on Jamie's side of the bed fools my subconscious into thinking he's beside me. This trick gives relief while I sleep.

Every morning, as I wake up my mind readjusts. Slowly, reality of Jamie's death returns.

Friends call often, "We're praying for you!"

"Thanks for the prayers. They're working. I made it through another day."

"Do you need anything?"

"No. Janet's still bringing meals. Thanks for the offer though. How can I pray for you?"

"Oh, Denise, my stuff isn't as big as yours. I don't want to bother you."

My soul hears God's prompting. "Tell them about your broken rib."

"Do you know I broke a rib the day after Jamie's brain surgery?"

"No, Denise, I didn't know! Are you okay?"

"Yeah, I'm fine. I only tell you now because compared to Jamie's surgery, the broken rib was nothing! But it still hurt like the dickens! It's the same way with prayer requests. Right now, yours may not seem as big as mine, but they still need prayer. Please let me pray for you!"

Thank You, Lord! That minor bump in our tumultuous world seemed so unnecessary at the time. Now, I see that You wanted to show me that all things need Your attention.

"Thank you, Denise. Yes, you can pray for…" Each caller shares their needs. Praying for others helps me focus on something other than my battle.

Despite occasional eruptions, serenity reigns in my heart. A friend stops in one day. We laugh as we recount memories. She asks, "Denise, you seem to have peace. How's that possible after all you've been through?"

God speaks through me, "I choose peace."

She contemplates the statement. "Choose peace."

"Yes, I can either choose to be distraught or choose peace, knowing God is in control. I deliberately choose peace."

About two months after Jamie's home-going, I attend lunch with John and his friends. He introduces me to a few people in the group. "This is my mom, Denise."

Each extends a warm welcome. "Hi, I'm…"

"Yeah, I'm John's mom."

"Where do you work?"

What do I say? I've always proudly said, "I'm a homemaker." What am I now?

These friendly folks seem confused by my silence, but they move on to other questions. We enjoy being out of the house. It feels good being invited into part of John's world.

After the lease on her rented house is complete, Shannon moves into my guest room. Having both kids home comforts me.

I don't know how John goes to work every day.

Our recent home videos keep me company as Shannon sleeps in every morning. Tears flow freely as I cherish each memory. Shannon and I weep, reminisce, and even laugh together. John sleeps late and then quickly leaves for his afternoon work shift. Shannon and I are usually deep asleep long before he gets home.

Our family's tension comes to a head one afternoon. The kids get into an ugly argument. The additional stress overwhelms me.

Trying to intervene, I stand between the two. The atmosphere's tense as I collapse wailing, "I've lost your dad. Now I'm losing my kids!"

Several months later, I fly to Little Rock to see my sister for a week. Needing rest, I sleep until noon every day. Cindy works half days and takes every afternoon off to spend time with me. We spend the evenings crying, praying and even laughing.

These days are a breath of fresh air, a glimpse back into "normal" life. Sister time replenishes my soul. We talk, really talk. We don't waste time with frivolous conversation. She's not only my sister by physical birth but also my sister in our Lord! All too soon, I fly home.

John picks me up at the airport. Mom made dinner for the three of us. We join hands after sitting around the table. I lead in prayer. "Lord, it's good to be home. Thank You for John and Shannon, for food and for Your goodness. Amen."

Shannon speaks softly, "Mom, we need to tell you something."

"What's up?"

"Well, I got really sick while you were gone."

"Uh-huh."

"I ended up being admitted to the University Hospital in Denver."

"Why didn't you call me?"

"Just listen, okay? The doctors told me that because of my ongoing pancreas problems, unless I have a transplant, I have two years to live."

Gulp. Blink. *Breathe. Slowly, breathe again.*

"Tell me about the transplant. Where do we have to go? Are you on a list?"

"Well…that's another thing. It's an experimental transplant. Because I have nerve damage in my stomach and lungs, and the kidney disease, I'm not a candidate for a normal transplant. There are three hospitals in the United States that do an experimental type of transplant. One is in California, one's on the east coast, and the other is in Tucson. That's the one I want to go to so it will be easier for you, John, and the grandparents to come see me. I've still got friends in

Phoenix and Uncle Bob lives there. Maybe some of you can stay with him. He's only two hours away from Tucson.

Two years to live, transplant, Tucson…

"And there's more, Mom, because it's experimental, insurance won't cover it. We need to raise $50,000 before I go to Tucson."

Fifty-thousand dollars! How much of the life insurance money do I have left after paying off the house? Why did I put the rest in an investment fund? I could sell the house, but where will we live? How quickly would it sell? What do I do with three households' belongings? Most of John's stuff is in the garage. Shannon's is in the borrowed moving trailer parked in the driveway. How will the three of us begin again?

The little energy I'd gained from my trip evaporates immediately. *Lord, what else? Why now? Be with us! Provide wisdom and money! Allow my girl to live!*

Shannon continues, "My Narcotics Anonymous group told me they'll help. Some of them have some money. We can do fundraisers. I'll make things to sell."

John interjects, "I'll work overtime and give what I can! I've got friends who'll help!"

Shannon adds, "Uncle Ron says he'll help too. He knows some people who own a restaurant. They're willing to have a fundraiser there."

My kids volley ideas and information back and forth. My shoulders creep toward my ears as muscles tense. *Lord, be with us! Help me breathe! Relax!*

John's soft voice interrupts, "I'll take time off to drive you to Tucson. If I need to, I'll get a job there."

I don't remember eating another bite. My head throbs from information and sorrow overload. "Thanks for telling me. Sorry I wasn't here when you found this out. Let's pray, okay?"

The three of us hold hands. "Lord, You know our needs. We ask You to guide us! Show us what we're supposed to do. Keep Shannon well enough to have the transplant. We're depending on You! Be our Strength, Peace, and Supplier! Lord, we need Your help. Line up the details for us. Provide the money. Provide the strength. Give us Your peace. Put everything in place…where to live, how to get there, the right doctors. Everything! In Jesus's name we pray. Amen."

The three of us talk for another hour. "Well, kids, I've got to get some rest. Hate to do this, but I'm heading to bed. Love you, night!"

Shannon states, "I'm not feeling too good. Think I'll turn in too. Love you, Mom, and you too, John. Goodnight!" She hugs me and then forces her brother to hug her. John, a night owl, stays up.

I thought life was a whirlwind before, but now, we are up against a ticking time bomb. Shannon's days are numbered!

Friends and friends of friends come out of the woodwork to help us raise money. Ronnie organizes a fundraiser at a local restaurant. I set up a special savings account for donated money.

John, extended family, and I study about the transplant in the next few days. We learn that during the pancreatic-islet-cell transplant, doctors will remove Shannon's pancreas, harvest healthy cells, remove and dispose of the organ, infuse the gleaned cells into her liver. Her liver will begin functioning as both liver and pancreas. As simple and as complicated as that!

Tonight, I have a terrifying nightmare. I dream someone's breaking into our house! My right hand automatically rises to tap Jamie's chest and immediately lands on the mattress. Reality hits me like a lead pipe. Fear overwhelms me. In the same moment I hear God whisper, "Don't be afraid or discouraged, I am the Lord your God. I will go with you wherever you go."

Peace floods through every pore.

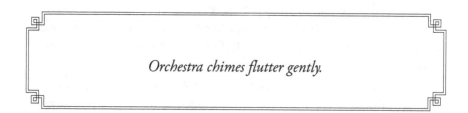

Orchestra chimes flutter gently.

25

Within nine months, we have the money. Knowing she'd need a vehicle in Arizona, Shannon asks her brother to drive her to Phoenix. The kids leave my house the following weekend. After hugging each one, I call out as they exit my house, "If you need me, call!"

John and Shannon spend the night at their Uncle Bob's house in Phoenix. John flies home the next day, leaving Shannon and her vehicle in Arizona. Shannon drives the two-hour trip from Phoenix to Tucson. Too exhausted to look further, she leases the first place she sees; a two-bedroom, two-bath apartment in a college-student neighborhood.

Thank You, Lord, that John had three days off so he could chauffeur his sister!

Shannon registers at the hospital the following day. While in Colorado, the Arizona's hospital staff was unwilling to set up appointments for her. Now, she has their full attention. Appointments are set and lab work scheduled as soon as possible. Shannon and I talk at least once a day.

Lord, be with her. You know her time is short! Give her strength to get groceries! Strength to cook! Strength to go to the hospital and make necessary calls! Protect her! Provide the IV supplies and meds she needs! I beg You to make things fall into place!

Almost four weeks later, Shannon calls while I'm getting groceries. She jokingly leaves the following message on my answering machine, "I want my mummy!"

Tears gently fill my eyes as I hear her voice. *I know she's being silly, but having her in Tucson alone is killing me!* I pick up the phone,

"Hello, I need to make airline reservations." Then I dial Shannon. "Hi, baby. Are you okay?"

"Yeah. Guess you got my message! I was just messing with you."

"Well, I'll be there next week."

"Mom, really, I'm okay."

"Shannon, really, I'm not. I just bought tickets."

Shannon's tone brightens with each phrase. "You're really coming? What day? What time?"

Okay, Lord. I'll be there till after her transplant. Tucson in the summer…me with MS. You know how heat makes my muscles tighten, vision double, strength disappear! Be with me!

A few days later, as I spend my daily time with the Lord, He leads me to Psalm 121:6 (NIV), "The sun will not harm you by day, nor the moon by night."[10]

Thank You, Lord! I'm claiming that as a promise from You to me! Thank You!

The flight to Tucson is without incident. Shannon picks me up at the airport then drives me to "our" apartment.

"Want me to drive for you to the apartment?"

"No, I'm fine. Just rest from the flight! We're not too far."

"That sounds good." My shoulders relax as I lean my head back against the headrest. Shannon's right, her apartment isn't far from the airport.

Tucson looks like a nice town. The city seems to be about the size Colorado Springs was in the 1970s.

"This is where I live and this is our assigned parking spot."

Gulp. "The apartment complex looks nice," I proclaim this as much to encourage my girl as myself. The three-story cinder block complex looms before me. I follow Shannon up the cement slab stairs to the second-floor landing.

The afternoon sun's heat embraces the west facing complex. Lord, it's not too bad in February, but I can't imagine how hot it will get in July.

We trek the narrow platform toting my luggage. Halfway down the complex's face, Shannon stops to open a door. "Here we are!" She beams with pride. I enter after her. "Here's a bathroom, there's the kitchen. This is the living room. The bedrooms and second bath are in the basement. Follow me, I'll show you which one is yours. Sorry about all the stairs. I rented the first furnished place I saw."

I gingerly make my way down the staircase. Because my MS causes my left leg to drag, stairs are difficult for me. I climb and descend them by putting one foot on the next step then the second foot joins it on the same stair. I repeat this until I reach the next level.

"This will be fine. I like the place. It'll be cooler having the bedrooms on a lower level."

"This is your bedroom. Look! You have two closets! Two college kids probably stayed in each room. Oh! See the art work I did to decorate! I used the brown paper off my medical supply boxes. I crumpled it up to look like leather and then straightened it out. I bought paint from the local dollar store and painted the designs. And I don't know if you noticed the end tables upstairs. I made those out of empty IV boxes!"

"Beautiful! You're so creative!" I smile. My heart and shoulders relax. *Thank You, Lord, for sustaining my girl. Jamie and I should've named her Joy. Your joy flows through her.*

Now, life consists of taxiing Shannon to doctor's appointments and gathering medical supplies and medicines to keep her alive. Weekly, I pile our laundry into grocery bags. I thread my left arm through them. Grabbing my cane with my right hand, I begin the l-o-n-g journey to the apartment's laundry facility.

My mind replays the route as I totter along. *Down two flights of stairs to the ground level, walk the width of the building; descend another smaller flight of stairs. Readjust the laundry, ouch! It's cutting into my arm! There, that's better. Almost there! Remember the door's code. Okay. We're there! Yeah!*

One day, after Shannon returns from a doctor's appointment, she informs me, "Mom, the money we raised is to pay for the surgery, but we need another fifty thousand dollars to pay the doctors!" *Lord, I have no way to raise the money, especially here in Tucson! I'm trusting You to provide.* His peace surrounds me.

The large room holds approximately twenty washers and dryers.

Okay. The sun will not hurt me…but no air conditioning? Seriously? I throw the laundry into the machines, check my watch, and retrace my steps. *Twenty-five minutes till they have to be thrown in the dryer. Get yourself "home" and get some cold water!* Laundry day takes every bit of my energy.

Thank You, Lord, that Your grace is new every morning!

This becomes a weekly expedition and challenge. *Okay, Lord, I need Your help! Give me strength!*

With each step I repeat these words:

> *The sun*
> *will not hurt*
> *you by*
> *day, nor*
> *the moon*
> *by night.*
> *Great is*
> *Thy faithfulness.*[11]
> *O God,*
> *my Father,*
> *There is*
> *no shadow*
> *of turning*
> *with Thee;*
> *All I*
> *have needed,*
> *Thy hand*
> *Hath provided;*
> *Great is*
> *Thy faithfulness,*
> *Lord, unto me!*
> *Thank You, Lord! We made it!*

*****

A few weeks before her surgery date, Shannon's doctor informs her, "The entire team of doctors has agreed to do the surgery for free. You owe nothing more than what you've already paid!"

Thank You, Lord! Only You could get twenty-three doctors to volunteer!

Shannon and I stay in the current apartment until the lease is completed. God prompts us to look for a more affordable, unfurnished place. I comb through local ads daily. We find a nice two bedroom/bathroom unfurnished duplex even closer to the hospital. The owner of our first apartment gives us two dressers. Shannon finds an inexpensive recliner online. The owners deliver it.

One afternoon, on our way back to the apartment we'll be leaving, Shannon sees a sign stating, "Hotel Furniture for Sale."

"Mom, why don't we stop in there and see what they have?"

"Sounds good to me!" Immediately, I swing into the business' parking lot. Inside we buy an entire hotel room full of furniture. For what we'll save on rent in two months, we buy two queen-sized beds with bedding, two-night stands, a small dining room table, four chairs, an entertainment center, a television, plates, bowls, silverware, and two pictures!

Shannon and I boast, "Wow! What incredible deals! They'll even deliver it to our new place next week! Isn't God good?"

The following week, Shannon finds a small couch for sale online for only $50. The owners agree to deliver it.

Excitedly, Shannon proclaims, "Everything will look great. Grandma and Grandpa will even have a bed when I'm in the hospital!"

Shannon sleeps most of the time. She only has enough energy to shower or wash her hair once a week. When awake, she busies herself crocheting or making duct tape purses. Her bent-at-the waist, habitually swaying back and forth posture almost seems normal. Shannon's nausea is so severe we've kept trash cans every five feet for the last two years. Our purses and vehicle have been stocked with bags for "emergency" eruptions. I'd kept a copy of Shannon's medical power of attorney in my handbag for the last year.

Lord, the things I've gotten used to as "normal life" are crazy! Yet somehow, I rarely think about them. I've calmly accepted it all. Thank You for Your peace. It really does go beyond my understanding!

On moving day, people from the church I've been visiting transfer our things to the new rental. *Thank You, Lord, for Your people!* The new couch arrives as men from the hotel sale bring furniture inside. Shannon and I collapse onto the couch after everyone leaves.

We only have two weeks before her transplant!

Lord, I'm excited about this surgery but know she might not live through it. Be with us! Be with me!

John and my parents drive down from Colorado the day before her surgery. Before we go to bed, Dad leads us all in prayer. As I lay in bed, I recall my discussion with my mom. "You and Dad can have my bed. Shannon and I will share a bed. John can sleep on the couch."

"No. You and Shannon need a good night's sleep before the surgery. We'll be fine on our air mattress."

End of discussion.

We all go to bed early. God allows sleep. Mom drives Shannon and me to the hospital. Dad and John will join us in about an hour.

People all across America are praying for my daughter, the doctors, and my family!

Shannon registers at the receptionist's desk. *I don't know how she's gained weight during the last year, but we've consistently gotten her larger and larger clothes! She's so weak and frail! Lord, be with her! Be with all of us!*

A nurse ushers us back to a preop room shortly after our arrival. "Here's your hospital gown. Let me see your bracelet the registrars gave you. Mm-hmm. Mm-hmm. Okay. When was the last time you ate?"

"Yesterday afternoon."

"Good. What type of surgery are you having?"

"A pancreatic islet cell transplant."

"All right. Do you have any questions?"

"No."

"Okay. The anesthesiologist will be in shortly, and then your surgeon."

We've been through this routine one too many times, Lord.

John pokes his head around the curtains, "Hi!" Shannon grins. "Come on in!" John and my parents enter. The five of us chat as the second hands on the clock slowly nudge toward surgery time. As promised, both the anesthesiologist and surgeon stop in, speak with Shannon, meet her family, and then exit.

Lord, it's only been a little over two years since we were all in Jamie's preop room.

Breathe, breathe. Be with us! Help her survive the surgery! Breathe. Straighten your back. Inhale. This scene has been repeated too many times. Blink back those tears. That's it.

Dad's gentle voice interrupts my thoughts. "Can I say a prayer before they take you?"

"Please!"

"Heavenly Father…" God's Spirit through Dad's prayer comforts my heart as well as quiets my soul.

I lean over and kiss my daughter's forehead, "Love you, honey! We'll see you after surgery!"

The nurse informs us before wheeling my girl away, "Someone will be out to give you updates throughout the surgery. Do you know where the waiting room is?" I nod. Wheeling my only daughter through the operating doors the nurse proclaims, "All right, this is it!"

Lord, be with her! Be with the surgeons! Let me see her alive again!

The orchestra's melody softens to a hush.
Once again, the Maestro's baton freezes in place.

26

John, my parents, and I do our best to occupy ourselves. *How do I read knowing what Shannon's going through? When will they stop her heart? When will they restart it? Lord, hold us all in Your loving arms! Help us get through today. Have today end in victory!*

Hours later, a nurse enters the waiting area. "Shannon's family?"

I stand immediately. "That's us!"

The professional swiftly makes her way to us. *Thank You, Lord, she's smiling!*

"The doctors have removed Shannon's pancreas. It's on its way to the facility where they'll harvest the good cells. Surgeons are continuing to work, moving everything to its new location. We have your phone number and will call if we need to reach you. Feel free to get some breakfast. This is going to be a very long day for you. We'll report to you again in a couple of hours."

"Thank you!" Mom and I hug. John's eyes glisten.

Mom opens her tote bag. "Who wants breakfast? I've got muffins, fresh fruit, and some juice. I noticed they have fresh coffee and hot water for tea in the corner."

Dad asks, "Why don't I say a prayer before we eat, then we can dig in!" The four of us hold hands. Dad prays, "Thank You, God for our food and we urge You to grant the doctors wisdom, Shannon health, and us peace. In Jesus's name we pray. Amen."

Eventually, another grinning nurse appears. "Hi, just reporting that everything is going as scheduled! The doctors are almost finished harvesting healthy cells from Shannon's pancreas. She's fine.

It's doubtful she will remember today. You are all doing great! We're about halfway there! Someone will be out to report to you in a couple of hours. Rest if you can!"

I stand and stretch. *Didn't notice how stiff my muscles have gotten! Feels great to move!*

Dad asks, "Denise, why don't you, John, and your mom get some lunch? I'll stay here."

John responds, "I'm going to stay here with you, Grandpa. Mom, you and Grandma go. We'll be fine. After you're back, we'll grab something."

"I hate to leave."

Mom puts her arm around me, "Let's go get lunch."

Reluctantly, I agree, "Okay."

After lunch Mom insists, "Let's go back to our room and take a nap. The guys are at the hospital and will call if they need us." I don't have strength to resist.

After twenty-three hours, a nurse informs us, "Shannon's in the recovery room. I'll let you know when you can see her. Then she'll be transferred to ICU."

We all breathe easier.

A short time later, a nurse opens the door. "Shannon's family?" She sees us and nods, "You can join her in the post-op room."

We excitedly gather our items, rushing to the door. *She's alive! Thank You, Lord!*

Shannon, obviously very medicated, tells the nurse, "I know I'm no doctor, but I don't think I need to go to ICU."

The nurse replies, "You're right. You're no doctor."

Lord, our girl is all right!

We trail behind the medical professional as she transfers Shannon to ICU.

Quickly, my eyes scan my daughter and the monitors. *Her color looks good, the machines show normal blood pressure, pulse-oxygen, temperature.*

The nurse coaches, "You may as well go home and rest. She'll probably sleep at least eight to ten hours." We follow her instructions.

*****

We spend the next two days in ICU with Shannon. Amazingly, although sore, her spirit's high. On the third day, after John and Dad leave to go back to Colorado, a nurse informs us, "Shannon's able to be moved to a regular room. We'll be moving her soon."

A regular room? Lord, please don't let her go to a "regular" room! She's still too sick and needs more care than she'll get in a regular room!

The nurse reappears, "Okay, we'll meet you on the fifth floor."

Lord, please provide good care!

Mom and I collect our things; follow the map to the elevators and ride up to the fifth floor. The sign "Transplant Floor" greets us. A huge sigh escapes my mouth.

Transplant Floor! Wish I'd known that was the floor they were talking about!

Shannon's "transplant team" of eighteen to twenty doctors make regular appearances. They question, probe, and applaud each milestone she passes.

Mom does her best to keep me out of trouble. I tell her, "Hospitals suck my brain out, leaving me in a state of chronic laughter."

We walk the halls taking pictures of anything I consider funny…a fire sprinkler over a fish tank, a fire alarm outside the hospital kitchen, a door marked, "This Door Must Remain Closed at All Times."

Really, why have a door if it's never opened?

Somehow, God gives me joy in this unnerving situation. Anything that can be misinterpreted is hysterical! I frequently laugh so hard I cry. After two and a half months, Shannon's released.

Mom and I stay in Tucson another six weeks, then my friend, Angel, flies out to stay with her until she's able to live alone.

Thank You, Lord, for providing support!

Mom drives us from Tucson to Colorado Springs not long after Angel arrives. *Being home feels so good!*

*****

The following fall, as I pull into my driveway, a song I've never heard plays on the car stereo, "Blessings" by Laura Story. Its words touch me so deeply I don't pull into the garage. Totally engrossed, I just sit, listen, and sob.

The next day I speak with Donna, "I heard the most amazing song yesterday, 'Blessings' by Laura Story!"

"Oh, I love that song! Do you know the story behind that song?"

"No."

"You've got to go online and hear why that song was written."

Later in the day, I do just that. More tears cascade down my cheeks as I learn the author of the song penned the lyrics as her husband dealt with brain cancer!

My church asks me to update them on Fearless Ministry a few weeks later.

My "mom brain" keeps me up many nights worrying about my girl.

Lord, I need help putting my thoughts onto trusting You!

"Where's there the most peace?"

In Your presence.

"Exactly! Concentrate on being in My presence."

I begin reciting Bible verses over and over in my mind. Several weeks later, as I lay in my dark bedroom concentrating only on God and His presence, suddenly a light shines so brightly it startles me! *Who turned the overhead light on?* Instincts open my eyes. The room is completely dark. *It was Your presence, Lord! Please allow me to experience that again, and not to startle!* God answers the prayer and grants the occurrence once again.

*****

In July, three years and seven months after Jamie's death, God asks me to write this letter to my parents:

Dad and Mom,

I had eighteen years as a child and thirty and a half years as a wife. I believe God is now calling me into a different ministry…probably mostly writing, sending cards and letters, maybe teaching a home ladies' Bible study!

You're concerned about who will take care of me when/if the MS progresses and as I grow older. You've both always taught that God will provide, and I'm not going to stop believing that now!

God's people have already stepped up and helped. Also... I'm not shy about asking! For the first time in over three and a half years I am excited about my future! God has given me peace that He has a plan for my life.

He is my Strength, my Shield, and He promises to be my Husband. God has a plan for the rest of my life and I'm now ready and excited to walk forward into it!

Love,
Denise

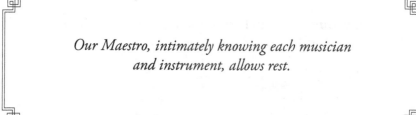

Our Maestro, intimately knowing each musician and instrument, allows rest.

27

Once Shannon's home the following winter, I'm relieved to have our family together. We each continue healing physically, emotionally, and spiritually.

God's been good to sustain us and guide us through Jamie's death and Shannon's surgeries. We've grown together and supported each other.

Shannon starts dating a nice man. They're engaged and married within only a few months.

I sense it's been difficult for John to be under my authority and roof. *Lord, it would be for any young man! Please provide a solution.*

After much prayer, I suggest, "John, what if I give you your inheritance, then you could put a down payment on your own place."

"You don't have to do that, Mom."

"I know, but I'd rather you have it now than after I die. What would you want in a house?"

"I'd want a bedroom, bathroom, kitchen, living room, and a two-car garage."

Typical guy response! "Okay, let's start praying and looking for your place!" His smile reveals the truth, he's relieved.

Lord, I bet John's been feeling stuck, like he was going to have to take care of me and his sister the rest of his life!

We look at several properties but none are right for my boy. Eventually, God shows us a property east of the city: a single-wide trailer with two bedrooms, two bathrooms, a living room, dining room, and a woodburning stove, located on five acres with a two-car garage, a three-car garage, and a carport!

John loves the place! He signs the contract the day we see it!

I see God working in each of our lives. John and Shannon are no longer children. I realize that He has a purpose for each of them, and I commit not to hold them back from following God's plan. Determined to allow my kids to have a good start in their new places, I tell them, "John, you can have the basement furniture, Shannon the den, and I'll take the living room."

Unified, I hear, "Thank you!"

SYMPHONY
MOVEMENT
NO. 5

28

After both kids move out, I realize this is the first time I've ever lived alone. I pull the car in the driveway, park; then enter my home. My shoulders relax. *I'm alone!* Inhaling deeply, I smile.

A few months later, I put the house on the market. I'm already praying about my next home. I occasionally drive through different neighborhoods looking.

My realtor takes me to several listings until I find a house and put a contract on it. It has the same floor plan of Jamie's and my house when our kids were little. Knowing my parents are just a few blocks away comforts me.

Lord, I think I'll be happy here, but it almost feels like I'm going backward in life instead of ahead. I'll have to change churches but I can probably go to my folks' church. Whatever's Your will is what I want.

My realtor calls a few days later, "Denise, the inspector found some problems I need to discuss with you. I'm emailing pictures of what he found."

"Okay… I've pulled them up."

"The first one is the inspection of the hot water heater. It's not installed to meet code. The second is the fuse box, it also doesn't meet code. The house wiring has been done wrong so the entire house needs to be rewired."

"Oh, boy."

"The next is a picture of the attic. Instead of insulation, there's shredded paper. In light of these findings, do you want to void the contract?"

"Yes, immediately!"

"Okay, figured that's what you'd say. Glad we got the house inspected!"

"Me too!"

The housing market's on fire! Houses often sell the day they're listed. Possible buyers continue to look at my current home. Daily, I pull up new listings. An interesting one shows up one morning. I call my realtor. "I want to see this place today."

"I'll pick you up in an hour."

Lord, the address looks close to a major road. I'm not sure about living there.

The realtor drives me into a small secluded townhome residence. I expect to hear traffic's roar, but instead peace and quiet embrace me as I exit the vehicle. I see a small cement patio. Peace washes over me.

That's where the bench the kids gave me to remember their dad will go. I know without going inside; this is my new home! I'll even be able to keep going to my church!

Every room in the townhome reveals exact desires of my heart. I put an offer on it promptly. My realtor calls the next day, "They accepted your offer!"

Okay, Lord, I trust You to send the right buyer for my current house.

Dad's wisdom convinces me to move in October "before the weather gets bad." Everything's packed and people from my church load and unload quickly. I'm moved in by noon. Every piece of furniture fits exactly where I'd planned. I continue sleeping at my previous house waiting for it to sell.

A couple comes in late October and signs the contract.

Thank You, God, but something about them doesn't feel right. The woman's excited; her husband doesn't want to move. He nitpicks about everything. I don't want to add to marriage problems. Have Your will done!

Their inspector finds major problems with my furnace. They cancel the contract stating,

"There's no way she'll pay that much to get it fixed."

Here we go again, Lord. You know how much this'll cost but it has to be done. Thank You for not selling our house to that couple. I trust You to work out all the details.

Good friends give me the name of a reliable furnace man; he comes and fixes the current problem. The next week I get a check from the IRS! I'd made a mistake on my taxes the previous year! *Of course, it's enough to pay for the furnace repair! Thank You, Lord!*

A couple falls in love with my house a few weeks later! They sign the contract; we quickly close!

My new place feels cozy. The neighborhood is quiet, isolated, and private. Mom continues coming to my place once a week. She helps me unpack, clean, and get groceries.

Thank You, Lord, for my new home and life. Allow me to bring glory to You! Lord, put people in my path for me to speak with about You.

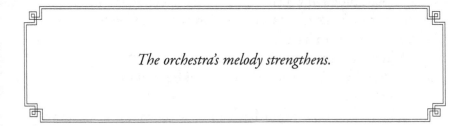

The orchestra's melody strengthens.

29

Several churches where Jamie spoke before his death ask me to share about the ongoing impact of "Fearless Ministry." I share at every opportunity how God is still opening doors for us to give law enforcement Bibles in which friends have highlighted some of Jamie's favorite verses. I ask for prayer that God will put together the video He instructed me to have made.

A man approaches me at church several months later. "My name is Randy. I heard you need help making a video."

"Yes, I do."

"I'm not an expert, but have a couple of months off between jobs and can work on it for you if you'd like."

"Absolutely!"

Randy edits, splices, and expertly adds music, graphics, and the logo to the video project.

*****

While picking up my mail in January 2017, I notice a man standing in the driveway of one of my neighbors. This property recently sold. After retrieving my letters, I drive to where the gentleman's standing. We talk briefly and introduce ourselves. I welcome him to the neighborhood.

The man, Floyd, shares that he bought the townhome and his daughter and son-in-law live in the basement. When he "is gone, they get the place." He shares that his daughter (my age) is a nurse and used to work for the police department. He is not only retired military, but also retired from Manitou Police Department. I mention that my late husband, Jamie Royal, was on CSPD. As I turn for home, I state, "I'd love to meet your daughter!"

They stop in the next day. His daughter, Linda, knew Jamie and his son-in-law, Steve, also met him during Jamie's duty at the Colorado Springs Airport. I state, "Oh! I have something to give you!" I retrieve two of the "Fearless Ministry" Bibles.

Both are thrilled with them. Over the next few months, whenever I see Floyd, he tells me, "I'm reading that Bible every day!"

I invite Floyd and Linda to visit my church. The two of them come, but Linda later shares that she has a church she attends. Floyd loves our church. He consistently mentions that he's never been in such a friendly group; he loves the preacher's "talks," and really likes the Bible class. Because he's in his late eighties, I attend a senior adult Bible study with him.

God allows me to not be able to drive most of this year. Floyd drives me to church every Sunday he goes! (I did ask Linda if his driving is okay. She said, "Yes. But if it ever isn't, let me know.") He frequently mentions, "If you need other rides, I can drive you!"

I ask God to show me where Floyd is in his spiritual walk. The first three weeks he attends church with me, he forgets his Bible. The fourth, he brings it. In Bible study, the teacher mentions to turn to Matthew, chapter 16. Floyd turns the first few pages in his Bible until he reaches the index. He looks up Matthew, and begins turning to that page number.

Thank You, Lord, for showing me where he is in his walk!

I begin praying for an opportunity to share the gospel with him. I ask if he could drive me to get groceries. He chauffeurs me; then we stop and buy takeout lunch. After he carries all my groceries inside, I say "If you have time, you can eat lunch here with me."

"I've got nothing but time!"

I pray before our meal. As we start eating, Floyd comments, "I need to ask you a question about the Bible. I asked Linda, but she told me to ask you. I believe in heaven and hell. What I wonder is, how do I know if I'm going to heaven or hell?"

Thank You, Lord, for this open door!

I share the plan of salvation verse by verse. Then I ask him, "Do you want to pray and ask God to forgive your sins and become the Lord/boss of your life?"

"Yes! But I'm not good at praying. That's why I don't say much in the Bible study. Everyone there knows all about the Bible. I don't."

"Well, Floyd, it's just you and me here. God doesn't care about what words you use. He just wants you to accept His free gift. Do you want to pray?"

"Well, that's a good question. Let's look in the Bible and see what God says. First, let's look at Romans 3:23. Will you read that to me?"

"Sure. For all have sinned and fall short of the glory of God."

"Good. Now, what does that mean?"

"That's easy! Everyone sins."

"That's right, now we'll look at Romans 6:23." I turn to that passage. "Will you read this also?"

"For the wages of sin is death, but the gift of God is eternal life through Christ Jesus our Lord."

"Good. What is a wage?

"It's what you get paid for something."

"Yes. What does the Bible say we get paid?"

He solemnly replies, "Death."

"That's right, but it means eternal death, separation from God. But what does the rest of the verse say?"

"The gift of God is eternal life through Jesus Christ our Lord."

"Exactly! God wants to give us eternal life! Now let's look at John 3:16. What does this say?"

"For God so loved the world that he gave his one and only Son, that whoever believes in him shall not perish but have eternal life."

"Let's look at a couple more verses. Now we'll turn to Ephesians 2:8–9. Please read them."

"For it is by grace you have been saved, through faith—and this is not from yourselves, it is the gift of God—not by works, so that no one can boast."

"If I give you a gift, but you never take it, is it yours?"

"Well, no. I guess not."

"One last verse, Revelation 3:20. Please read this on."

"Here I am! I stand at the door and knock. If anyone hears my voice and opens the door, I will come in and eat with that person, and they with me."

"Jesus is offering you the gift of eternal life. Are you ready to ask Jesus to forgive your sin, and become your Lord and Savior?"

"Yes, but I'm not a good pray-er."

With that, he gently reaches across the table to hold my hand and prays, "God, I know I sin. Thank You for Jesus who died and rose from the dead. Please forgive my sin and come into my life. Amen."

He's now daily reading "Jesus Calling."

Thank You, Lord, for showing that You're not finished with me!

*****

A few months later, God opens the doors for making the jamieroyalfearlessministry.com website a reality!

Lord, I'd really like to have this interpreted into American Sign Language. If that's Your will, please help it happen.

A woman approaches me after church a month later. "Denise, I heard you're hoping to have the video interpreted into ASL. Here's a check to pay an interpreter."

The check covers all but $15 of the expense. One of our pastors films the endeavor. It's soon added to the website.

The following spring, I speak at my church about Fearless Ministry's progress. A young police officer also shares about his newly launched ministry, Shield616. We compare details with each other while cleaning our tables off. He asks, "So your ministry gives Bibles to police officers?"

"Yes, sir, we sure do."

"Well, my vision's for Shield616 to give Bibles to law enforcement. What if we combined our ministries?"

"I'd love that!"

Because their Bible publisher cherishes the concept, they print labels detailing Fearless Ministry and sharing our website's address.

The following year his publisher, Biblica, makes "Thin Blue Line" Bibles specifically for Shield616 and law enforcement. They even leave a blank page inside for information about Fearless Ministry.

Lord, only You can do the impossible!

*****

Opening my email in the autumn of 2019, I see thirty-four unread messages. *Ugh!* I quickly scan the addresses deleting ones I don't recognize. *Good. That leaves only eighteen.*

I deliberately save one post to read last. My mouse cursor hovers over the link.

This address looks vaguely familiar. Wonder if Marilyn changed her address?

Cautiously, I open the message. Several advertisements immediately appear on my screen. *Nope. Not from Marilyn.*

Quickly, I put the message in my computer's trash bin. I leave my desk to complete other tasks.

My computer's sluggish later in the day. *This thing's as slow as a sloth! I may as well shut it down till tomorrow.* I yawn deeply, happy it's bedtime!

I restart my computer the following morning. The machine wakes at a tortoise's gait. The screen eventually responds. Advertisements display across the screen.

Oh no! That's not good! Better call my computer's security service!

I dial their phone number. "Hello, I need help. My computer might have a virus."

An American man's voice comforts my ear. "I'm sorry to hear that. Let me connect you with someone who can help."

"Thank you."

I hear a few clicks before a woman with a foreign accent answers. My eyebrows prejudicially rise.

"Hello, my name is Alice. How can I help?"

"I need you to see if my computer is infected with a virus."

"Oh, I hope it does not have a virus. Do I have your permission to take control of your computer?"

"Yes." I somberly observe my monitor. Program after program open on my screen.

Alice speaks again, "Ma'am? Are you still there?"

"Yes, just watching my computer."

"Ah, yes. I am opening different programs on your computer. I do see several things that need to be fixed. You have gotten a very bad virus. I will have to completely wipe your computer clean. It will only have what it had when you bought it. Are you okay with this?"

My heart sinks. "Yeah, go ahead and do what you need to do."

"Do you have everything saved that you want to keep?"

God prompts my mind. "Your most important documents are on CDs."

Thank You, Lord, for reminding me about them!

With renewed peace, I relinquish control to the Indian woman. "Yes, I have everything I need."

"Okay, this will take a long time, maybe two hours. You can leave your office if you have other things to do. Please come back every fifteen minutes so I can give you a progress report."

"Thank you. I'll be right back." I return to my desk five times during the next ninety minutes. The last time I ask, "Ma'am, I'm back. Are things any closer to being fixed?"

"Yes, ma'am. You had a very bad virus. I apologize. These problems take a long time to correct."

"I appreciate your help."

"Okay. Now we just have to wait for my computer to finish with your computer. I am sorry for the inconvenience."

Hmm, if she's just sitting there, and I'm just sitting here, wonder if she'd like to practice her English?

"While we're waiting…what's the weather like today in India?"

"Yes! I live in India! Mumbai, India! We are having our rainy season. It normally takes me two hours to get to work. Now it takes me three, sometimes four, hours."

"Wow! That makes a long day for you!"

"Yes, a long day, but I am thankful to have work. Where do you work?"

"I'm disabled, so I don't work."

"I am very sorry you are disabled."

"Thank you, but I'm fine."

"Are you married?"

"No. My husband died seven years ago."

"So sorry, ma'am!"

"Thank you, but I'm fine."

"Do you have any children?"

"Yes. I have a son and a daughter. Both live close to me."

"That is very good."

"My daughter had a transplant five years ago. Some of her doctors are from India."

"Is she okay now?"

"She's fine." *Still on a day-to day,* "living by God's grace" *existence, but she's alive.*

"I am happy that she is okay. I am sorry, but I cannot finish the job on your computer today. Can we make an appointment for 9:00 a.m. Wednesday morning?"

"Yes."

Two mornings later, I glance at my clock when I hear my phone ring.

It's only eight fifty. The computer company's calling a few minutes early.

The phone's caller ID displays my daughter's name. "Hi, Girlie, how're you today?"

She weakly responds, "Well, I'm at the emergency room at the hospital."

"I'll be there as soon as I can!"

Lord, be with her and the doctors!

My phone rings again before I leave the house. This time the caller ID shows the computer repair service. I grab the receiver. "Hello."

"Hello, this is Alice. Is this Mrs. Royal?"

"Yes, it is."

"We have an appointment this morning. Will this still work for you?"

"No, I'm sorry. My daughter is in the emergency room at the hospital. I'm on my way to her."

"Oh! I am so sorry. I hope your daughter will be okay. Can we reschedule for Saturday morning around nine? I hope your daughter will be all right."

Unexplainable peace flows into me. God speaks words through me I don't yet feel. "She'll be fine. My God is the Great Physician. I will plan to speak to you Saturday morning."

I spend my regular time with God in prayer and Bible study Saturday morning. Expecting the computer repair service's call any moment, I enter my home office. God stirs my heart before I sit in the office chair.

"Kneel and pray about today's conversation with the lady from India."

The phone rings as I finish praying. I lift the receiver and gently answer, "Good morning."

"Hello. This is Alice. Is this Mrs. Royal?"

"Yes, it is. How are you this morning?"

"How is your daughter?"

I smile. *God, You've kept us on this woman's mind.* His peace once again encompasses me. "She's fine."

"Is she out of the hospital?"

"Yes, thanks for your concern."

"I am so happy to hear she is okay! Do you want to finish with your computer?"

"Yes, I'm at my computer, ready for you to take control."

Alice completes the process within thirty minutes. "Mrs. Royal, everything has been accomplished. Do you have any other questions?"

"Yes, just one. I'm a praying person. I'm wondering if you have anything you'd like me to pray about?"

Silence hangs between us like an exhaled breath on a winter day. "Well, my husband and I are trying to have a baby. Would you pray about that?"

"Yes, I will pray about that. Thank you for sharing that with me."

"Um… Mrs. Royal…" Alice's voice now quivers.

I wonder if she's trying not to cry!

"There is…something…else…"

"Okay, what else can I pray about?"

"Ma'am…we've talked…three…times."

I laugh, "Yeah, three times in one week!" Alice isn't laughing.

Almighty God, I feel that You're up to something! Guide my words.

He reminds me of facts I've learned about India: most people in India are Hindu, therefore have many "gods," most with higher paying jobs learned English while attending Catholic schools.

Alice's trembling voice draws my mind back to our conversation. She softly continued, "Ma'am…every…time…we…talked… you have…peace."

"Yes, I do have peace."

"I…ah… I…want…your…peace. Would you…pray…that I can…have your peace?"

"Yes, I will, but to have my peace, you have to have my God. Did you go to a Catholic school?"

"Yes. Yes, I did."

"Do you know that Jesus is God's Son?"

"Yes."

"Do you know that Jesus died on the cross and three days later arose alive?"

"Yes, I do."

"Well, to have my peace, you have to ask my God to be your God. Your only God. Are you willing to do that?"

"Yes."

"Right now?"

"Yes, but…in…my…heart. Please…give…me…a few…moments."

"Certainly."

She states seconds later, "I…did…what…you said…but… I…don't…ha… Oh! Yes! I do! I have peace!"

"I'm so happy for you! My God is now your God!"

Her voice resumes a professional tone. "If you have no other questions about your computer, may I close your case?"

"Yes."

"Ma'am, to close your case, you will need to speak with my supervisor."

"That's fine."

"He'll be on the phone next."

A man's Indian accent resounds immediately. "Mrs. Royal? This is Paul speaking. I…noticed…my…"

Lord, he sounds like he's trying not to cry! Are you moving in his heart too? Did he hear our conversation? Did he pray when Alice prayed?

Paul continues, "My employee…becoming emotional…so… uh… I…listened…"

God's delight embraces me. I reply, "Sir, I'm glad you listened. I will pray for you."

"Thank you!" He clears his throat. "Are we finished fixing your computer?"

"Yes, sir."

"I will close your case then. Have a good day."

"I will! Goodbye!"

My smile broadens. *Lord, You're incredible! What Satan meant for evil, You turned to good! Thank You for the computer virus and transferring my call to India! You allowed a disabled widow in the US to introduce two people in India to You! My transferred call was actually Your opportunity!*

Cymbals, rejoicing resound as the Maestro nods acknowledging His appreciation.

30

At the 2019 Cotton Bowl in Texas, Shield616 presents shield packages containing Bibles with Fearless Ministry's information to new police officers!

Lord, You really can do more than we ask, think, or imagine! Thank You!

Our church is rapidly growing and branching out. We recently "adopted" a smaller church to help them. The women I've been involved with need to find Bible study classes. Hoping to narrow down choices, I attend the Women's Life Group and enjoy it so much I plan to join it and maybe ask one of the young ladies to join as well. But as I pray, God brings two other young women to my mind. Where will they go? God nudges me to attend the class Jamie and I used to attend. Both women agree they'd attend with me.

I call them the following afternoon. "What'd you think of the class?" Both loved it. God's peace settles over me.

Thank You, Lord, for taking care of these precious sisters.

As I relax later in the afternoon, a fresh wave of release washes over me.

Wonder what this peace is from? I didn't think I was burdened. Maybe I was though.

Thoughts of yesterday play through my mind as I climb out of bed the next morning.

Yes, it sure was a good day. I enjoy being in my old class. It feels like home.

"Yes, but that isn't the place for you. You're to go to the new location. Don't think of former things."

But, Lord, what do I have to add? What can I do to help at a new place?

During my quiet time with my Lord, He leads me to 1 Corinthians 12. He reminds me that He puts His body together just as He wants.

Yep. I know that, Lord.

I continue reading, 1 Corinthians 12:22b seems to be written in highlights: "Those parts of the body that seem to be weaker are indispensable" (NIV).[12]

Weaker things? Really? Incredible. Only in Your hands!

Then He takes me to another Bible study. Today's lesson is about stepping out in faith. By being obedient we get to know more of God's power.

Lord, I'm so excited! Okay, I'm going forward! Yesterday's peace was you releasing me from my last church. Thank You for being faithful, always going before me! You've been my Guide, Comfort, and Deliverer throughout my life...and You will continue to be!

Concerts continue throughout the years.
The Maestro faithfully conducts His orchestra,
patiently working with each instrument.
Just when I think I've mastered the desired technique,
He introduces a new challenge.
The music ebbs and flows,
each note is as important as each rest.
The audience gives a standing ovation.
The Maestro bows.

DENISE'S COMMENTS

Thank you for reading God's story through my life. I hope you have a growing personal relationship with my Lord, Jesus Christ. Only through Him, His power, and His grace am I able to face each day. He provides strength and hope. His mercies are new every morning. He wants you to more than just survive!

If your life has not had as many positive turns and twists as mine, I encourage you that God is not finished with your story! Ask God to open your eyes to what He is doing around you and how you can join His work.

I encourage you to read Hebrews 11. That chapter is often called the chapter about "heroes of the faith." Verses 1–35 do list many of these godly men and women, but keep reading Hebrews 11:36, 12:2:

> Others suffered mocking and flogging, and even chains and imprisonment. They were stoned, sawn in two, they were killed with the sword. They went about in skins of sheep and goats, destitute, afflicted, mistreated—of whom the world was not worthy—wandering in deserts and mountains, and in dens and caves of the earth.
>
> And all these, though commended through their faith, did not receive what was promised, since God had provided something better for us that apart from us, they should not be made perfect.

Therefore, since we are surrounded by so great a cloud of witnesses, let us also lay aside every weight, and sin which clings so closely, and let us run with endurance the race that is set before us, looking to Jesus, the founder and perfecter of our faith, who for the joy that was set before him endured the cross, despising the shame, and is seated at the right hand of the throne of God.

*****

We usually do not see the end of the book until we reach heaven! Hold onto our Lord. Trust that He does want what's best and promises to be with you through everything!

I hope and pray that you know The Maestro. It's as easy as A, B, C!

- Admit you've sinned.
- Believe that Jesus died for you and rose again on the third day.
- Ask God to forgive your sin, commit your life to Him as your Lord/Boss.
- Welcome to His family!

If you have a family member or loved one who is walking through difficult times, do the following:

- ✓ Spend time with them IF they want you to be with them. Be sensitive to their needs.
- ✓ Those in crisis mode often need help with simple tasks— laundry, cooking, paying bills, etc.
- ✓ Don't worry about what to say. Sometimes it's best to just be quiet.

- ✓ Ask them over or out for a meal. Often, they miss being with families or other couples.
- ✓ Give your talent, and time and presence. *(If you're not able to be with them physically, contact them in other ways.)*
- ✓ Listen! Allow them to ooze their grief. It may be messy for a time, but be long-suffering with them.
- ✓ Support their decisions. It's helpful to allow them to talk through their thought process. Guide gently with godly wisdom "let your speech be seasoned as with salt."
- ✓ Pray for God to guide them. It's okay if they go through an angry spell.
- ✓ Watch for signs of prolonged depression.
- ✓ It's fine to remember fun memories! End those precious times of tears and laughter with prayers of praise for the time they enjoyed together!

DON'T

Don't preach. Now is the time for listening.

Don't put a time limit on their grief. The absence of a loved one is not something one can "just get over!" God's healing pours over each in His timing. He is capable and desiring to woo them back to Himself.

Don't speak poorly of their loved one.

Don't be surprised if their mind is foggy for the first few years. This is often the case.

(I believe God protects by placing a temporary numbness over them as they heal.)Don't be alarmed by their desire to date or not date. God will let them know if and when the time comes for a new relationship.

In the meantime, "weep with those who weep, rejoice with those who rejoice!"

ACKNOWLEDGMENTS

First and foremost, I thank God Who is my life! Without His direction and instruction, this book would have not been written. May this be a tribute to Him alone.

Thank You, Lord, for revealing Your plan through Your word by personalizing Deuteronomy 8:2b, "You led me all the way...these forty years to humble and test...to know what is in my heart."

I also thank others who've walked this path by my side.

- I begin with my parents, Pat and Alma Pattison. Thank you for teaching me of a loving God and the importance of prayer. My sister, Cindy, and brother, Roger, who've encouraged and helped along the way. My mother-in-law, Terri Royal, thank you for teaching me to relax in His grace. My children, John and Shannon, thank you for being precious Guinea pigs. (Mothers don't get a practice run!) Also, my friend, cousin, and editor, Robbi.
- My dear friend, Angel, you walked alongside me through my darkest days and still love me!
- My good friend, Donna, you taught me that God gives the grace I need at just the exact moment it's required.
- My faithful friend, Kathy, you taught me that singleness doesn't limit how God can and will use a person.
- The Grace Prayers, under June's guidance. You've provided spiritual CPR more often than I can count.
- The Writing Creation group, you've encouraged, educated, honed my skill and been my cheerleading team. Alane, for inviting me to join the group; Judy, for graciously host-

ing our meetings; Carole, for faithfully setting an example; Renee, for not only bringing a professional touch, but also laughter; Esther, graciously guiding, and Karen for sharing in our love of writing.

- And my brothers in blue: Michael, Ronnie, Gary, Buck, and Mark.

For all who don't find your name within these pages, know if your choruses hadn't mingled with mine, my melody wouldn't be as full.

NOTES

[1] Thomas Andrew Dorsey, lyrics for "Precious Lord, Take My Hand" (sung by Evie Tornquist Karlsson and others).

[2] Brent Lamb and John Rosasco, "Household of Faith" (sung by Steve and Marijean Green).

[3] "I Expect a Miracle" (sung by Bill Gaither Trio).

[4] Henry Blackaby, Experiencing God: Knowing and Doing the Will of God.

[5] Anne Graham Lotz, The Vision of His Glory.

[6] Bill and Anabel Gillham, video set "The Life," now available as a DVD set.

[7] Bruce Wilkinson, The Prayer of Jabez: Breaking Through to the Blessed Life.

[8] Ray Boltz, "Thank You for Giving to the Lord."

[9] Kim Noblitt, lyrics for "If You Could See Me Now."

[10] Psalm 121:6 NIV.

[11] Thomas O. Chisholm, hymn lyrics for "Great Is Thy Faithfulness."

[12] 1 Corinthians 12:22b NIV.

ABOUT THE AUTHOR

Spending time with her Lord, encouraging others, and prayer are her top priorities. Her writing and public speaking continues. She lives a quiet, content life while staying active in her local church. Her children and parents live close. God continues answering her prayer as she does far more than "just survive!"